For Linda Cooper and Beryl Shardlow

Knowledge is power.

(Nam et ipsa scientia potestas est.)

Francis Bacon. 1561-1626

European Social Work Publications from Russell House Publishing

In this series

Adams, A., Erath, P. and Shardlow, S. M. (eds) (2000) *Key Themes in European Social Work: Theory, Practice, Perspectives.*

Adams, A., Erath, P. and Shardlow, S. M. (eds) (2000) *Fundamentals of Social Work in Selected European Countries: Historical and Political Context, Present Theory, Practice, Perspectives.*

Other titles

Aluffi-Pentini, A. and Lorenz, W. (Eds.) (1996) *Anti-racist Work with Young People: European Experiences and Approaches.*

Barrett, D. (Ed.) (2000) *Youth Prostitution in Europe: A Problem out of Control?*

Cooper, A. et al. (1995) *Positive Child Protection: A View from Abroad.*

Hetherington, R. et al. (1996) *Protecting Children: Messages from Europe.*

Lindstein, T. and Metyard, B. (1996) *What Works in Family Mediation: Mediating Residence and Contact Disputes.*

Patel, N. et al. (1998) *Dementia and Minority Ethnic Older Persons: Managing Care in the UK, Denmark and France.*

Journal

Social Work in Europe. Three issues per year. Edited by Patrick Ayre and Rachael Hetherington.

A BIBLIOGRAPHY OF EUROPEAN STUDIES IN SOCIAL WORK

Steven Shardlow

and

Stacey Cooper

RHP

Russell House Publishing

First published in 2000 by:
Russell House Publishing Ltd.
4 St. George's House
Uplyme Road
Lyme Regis
Dorset DT7 3LS

Tel: 01297-443948
Fax: 01297-442722
e-mail: help@russellhouse.co.uk

British Library Cataloguing-in-publication Data:
A catalogue record for this book is available from the British Library.

ISBN: 1-898924-53-8

Typeset by Steven Shardlow and Stacey Cooper

Printed by Hobbs, Totton, Hants

Contents

Preface

This book is one result of three years of co-operation by a multinational group, sponsored by the Socrates programme of the European Union. The initial aim of the group was to develop and then implement, in the curricula of their respective educational institutions, a common module on Theories and Models of Social Security Systems and Social Work Practice in Europe.

Inevitably, in such a time consuming and demanding project, not all European countries could be taken into account; nevertheless, the group does include representative examples from a range of different models of social security systems across Europe.

One result of the work of the group has been to produce three books. First, a book that explores the historical and political contexts of social work in several European countries. Second, a book that builds upon this and provides critical analysis of important themes in social work across Europe. Third, this book, a bibliography of materials published in English about social work in Europe. These publications are intended to complement each other in the development of understanding about social work across Europe, and to promote better practice through the exchange and sharing of ideas.

During this programme of work, there has been an active exchange of lecturers and students from the participating universities within the framework of a student and staff mobility programme.

The materials that comprise this book, emerged from a process of continuous development, discussion and refinement by the group. They have been devised to assist social work students with an interest in the European dimension of social work and those who undertake visits abroad as part of their studies, or for other professional reasons.

However, these three texts are not solely aimed at students. Practitioners, managers and policy makers in the constituent countries cannot afford to ignore the ways in which social work practice is developing elsewhere in Europe. Hence, this book is intended to assist current debates about policy and practice by providing a starting point for the identification of information about social work in Europe.

It has not been possible to represent all countries in Europe within such a volume. There is an imbalance in that the majority materials are about countries that are part of the European Union. None-the-less there has been a deliberate attempt to include examples of social work as practised in very different welfare regimes.

Adrian Adams, Canterbury Christ Church University College

Peter Erath, The Catholic University of Eichstatt

Steven Shardlow, The University of Sheffield

Also by Steven Shardlow

Doel, M., and Shardlow, S. M. (1993) *Social Work Practice*. Aldershot: Gower.

Doel, M., and Shardlow, S. M. (1998) *The New Social Work Practice*. Aldershot: Arena.

Doel, M., and Shardlow, S. M. (eds.) (1996) *Social Work in a Changing World: An International Perspective on Practice Learning*. Aldershot: Arena.

Doel, M., Shardlow, S. M., Sawdon, C., and Sawdon, D. (1996) *Teaching Social Work Practice*. Aldershot: Arena.

Shardlow, S. M. (ed.) (1989) *The Values of Change in Social Work*. London: Routledge.

Shardlow, S. M., and Doel, M. (1996) *Practice Learning and Teaching*. Houndmills, Basingstoke: Macmillan.

Shardlow, S. M., and Payne, M. (eds.) (1998) *Contemporary Issues in Social Work: Western Europe*. Aldershot: Arena.

About the authors

Steven Shardlow is Director of Social Work Studies at the University of Sheffield, UK. Previously he has worked as a social work practitioner and manager in both field and residential work. He is ex-chairperson of the Association of Teachers in Social Work Education (UK) and Editor of the Journal of Social Work (a new journal to be published by Sage in 2001). In addition, he is a member of the Executive Committee of the European Association of Schools of Social Work, representing the UK.

He has been involved in international social work, particularly in Europe through development work, consultancy and research. Current research and teaching interests are in the following areas: social work values and ethics; comparative social work practice; social work education especially practice learning. He has published widely in these fields and his work has been translated into several languages.

Stacey Cooper is a research assistant and is studying for a PhD at the University of Sheffield.

Acknowledgements

A large number of people are involved in the production of any book, this is no exception. Many of the names go unrecorded but we would like to thank the staff at Russell House who have been enthusiastic and helpful as this book, and the project of which it forms a part, have developed. We would also like to extend our thanks to the following who have influenced the development of the ideas in this book and helped in its compilation: Adrian Adams, Oldrich Chytil, Monserrat Feu i Closas, Peter Erath, Rino Fasol, Willi Fischges, Jordi Sabater i Garcia, Juha Hämäläinen, Emmanuel Jovelin, Geert van der Laan, Wolfgang Klug, Pauli Niemelä, Radka Popelková, Horst Sing, Evelyne Tully and Francesco Villa.

We also wish to thank the European Union without whose financial support this book would not have been possible. The EU has provided the opportunity for us to come together as a group, through mobility programmes and enabled us to build good working relationships.

As ever, the authors of the book gratefully acknowledge the help of others but accept responsibility for the books contents - including any mistakes!

Future Editions

Steven Shardlow would be pleased to receive details of further works which readers consider might usefully be included in future editions of this bibliography. Please send them to:

Department of Sociological Studies

The University of Sheffield

e-mail: S.Shardlow@sheffield.ac.uk

Introduction

The scope of the bibliography

The idea for this bibliography of European studies in social work was developed during collaborative work across several European countries to produce a common teaching and learning module in European social work. The bibliography is designed for all those who have an interest in European social work and who want to identify relevant published materials.

Like all bibliographies the scope of this one has been limited by a range of factors including: the methods of searching for the materials, the databases used, the key terms used and so on. Most importantly, some constraints have been consciously placed on the scope of the bibliography.

Perhaps the single most significant limitation is that it is restricted to materials that have been published in English. The inclusion solely of English materials was pragmatic, as English is one of the most commonly used languages and widely spoken within Europe. This fact should not be taken to imply that materials published in other languages are not just as valuable as those included in this bibliography.

Only materials published after 1980 have been included (with the exception of dictionaries). Earlier materials would not generally be of central concern for the current practice of social work in Europe. Nor are such materials likely to be abundant or easy to identify.

The bibliography has been designed to include:

- comparative studies of social work that include at least two European states;
- comparative studies of social work that include at least one European state compared with at least one non-European state;
- general theoretical material on comparative studies in social work;
- single country studies that are of particular value and interest to those living outside that country.

The search failed to locate a pre-existing bibliography relating to social work in Europe.

The Search

Compiling a bibliography always entails some difficult choices, in particular where to search for published materials and which terms to use as 'key words' for the search. After a careful process of reviewing the most common keywords used by the major social work journals, we determined on the following list of key terms to define the parameters of social work.

Aged
Care
Capitalist societies
Child abuse
Child advocacy
Child neglect
Child protection
Child welfare
Children
Children's rights
Community care
Community services
Comparative research
Comparative social work
Comparative theory
Comparing
Contrasting
Crime
Criminal
Cross cultural studies
Cross national research
Cross national studies
Delinquency
Delinquent
Developed nations
Disability
Disabled
Drug
Drug abuse
Drug misuse
Education
Elderly
Empirical research
Empirical studies
Europe
European social work
European Union
European welfare
Families
Handicap
Human services
International education
International social work
Juvenile offenders
Learning difficulties
Mental health
Mentally ill
Offenders
Old age
Paedophile
Paedophilia
Parents
Pensions
Professional education
Schizophrenia
Siblings
Social agencies
Social problems
Social science research
Social services

Social work
Social work diploma
Social work education
Social work qualification
Social workers
Socrates
Statutory social work
Voluntary agencies
Voluntary social work
Welfare
Welfare agencies
Welfare payments

Defining the boundaries of Europe is not an easy matter, as Lorenz has suggested many different 'Europes' have existed throughout the ages from the 'pax Romana', to the economic, political and social Europe of the European Union (Lorenz, 1994). However, we have included the following countries as part of the search:

Albania
Andorra
Armenia
Austria
Belgium
Bulgaria
Corsica
Croatia
Cyprus
Czech Republic
Denmark
Estonia
Finland
France
Germany
Greece
Hungary
Irish Republic
Italy
Latvia
Liechtenstein
Lithuania
Luxembourg
Macedonia
Moldova
Monaco
Netherlands
Norway
Poland
Portugal
Romania
Russia
Serbia
Slovak Republic
Slovakia
Slovenia
Spain
Sweden
Switzerland
Turkey
Ukraine
Yugoslavia

Using the 'keywords', the following databases were searched for relevant material from 1980 until 1999.

Bids ISI
Bids IBSS
British Education Index
British Humanities Index
Caredata
Dissertation Abstracts
Eric Literature Database
Index to Theses
International Eric
International Political Science Abstracts
Internet
Psychlit
Social Science Index
Star (Library Database)
Social Science Citation Index

References acquired through conducting general searches on the Internet were frequently incomplete, including occasional omissions of the author's name! The necessity to check the accuracy of details and complete imperfect references contributed to making this the most time consuming part of the search.

The framework developed to group citations altered significantly as the literature search progressed. Original categories included: empirical comparative studies, general non-empirical studies, theory of comparative social work, single country studies, social work education, bibliographies, dictionaries and a more general social work in Europe. This was accompanied by a number of sections divided into areas of social work's professional practice: children and families, old age, offenders, mental health, and learning difficulties.

The number of categories was reduced by either merging sections together or removing the section altogether due to lack of material to include therein.

Placing references in appropriate categories, particularly those unaccompanied by an abstract, was at times problematic. There remains an element of overlap within sections, which combined with the arbitrary nature of some titles contributed to a time consuming evaluation of placing some of the references.

Organisation of the bibliography

The final organisation of the bibliography is in two major sections. The first includes comparative studies, i.e. those materials where there is a significant juxtaposition of two or more countries. The second section contains materials where the primary focus is upon a single country but where that material would be of interest to non-residents who are seeking information about some aspect of social work. A final smaller section includes dictionaries. It is highly likely that there are more of these but our searches failed to reveal them. To assist with finding materials we have included an index of countries, this index indicates some of the major items that refer to a particular country in the abstracts. It does not identify every country referred to in each of the published materials included in the bibliography – this would be beyond the scope of the present work.

Each of the major sections is organised by client groups. This organisation does not necessarily lead to a neat and tidy division. We hope that if, as a reader, you think an entry is incorrectly classified, you will be tolerant of our attempts to bring order to very diverse materials.

All bibliographies involve some degree of selection. All are incomplete in some respects. This one is no different. It is designed to help those who are seeking information about social work in Europe. We hope it provides that help.

Comparative studies

Children and families

Anglin, J. P. (1990) 'Editorial: emerging international perspectives', *Child and Youth Care Quarterly* 19: 73-4.

Barth, R. P. (1992) 'Child welfare services in the United States and Sweden: different assumptions, laws and outcomes', *Scandinavian Journal of Social Welfare* 1(1): 36-42.

The child welfare systems in Sweden and the United States were dramatically reformed beginning in the early 1980s. After ten years, the different results of these reforms are quite striking. These child welfare systems have different methods of preserving families in crisis; different assumptions about the role of birth parents, foster parents, and adoptive parents; and different goals for children who will not go home. Each of these areas is explored and recommendations made for re-examining child welfare services in both countries.

Bradshaw, J., Ditch, J., Holmes, H. and Whiteford, P. (1993) *Support for Children: A Comparison of Arrangements in Fifteen Countries*, London: Department of Social Security/HMSO.

Research study comparing the structure and level of benefits for families with children.

Bradshaw, J. et al. (1993) 'A comparative study of child support in fifteen countries', *Journal of European Social Policy* 3(4): 255-271.

Reports on a study of the child support package in all countries of the European Community, Australia, Norway and the United States of America. The UK package overall is ranked towards the middle of the league table of countries. It tends to be ranked higher in its package for low-paid lone parents and couples, and where comparisons are made after housing costs. It tends to be ranked lower in its package for large families, families with a pre-school child requiring care and lone parents and children and couples with children dependent on income support.

Bradshaw, J., Ditch, J., Holmes, H. and Whiteford, P. (1993) *Support for Children: A Comparison of Arrangements in Fifteen Countries*. London: Department of Social Security, HMSO.

Research study comparing the structure and level of benefits for families with children.

Calder, M. (1997) 'Young people who sexually abuse: towards an international consensus', *Social Work in Europe* 4(1): 36-39.

Describes the evolution of the problem of young people who sexually abuse and calls for international collaboration to contribute to a more speedy and effective resolution of this problem.

Cavadino, P. (ed.) (1996) *Children Who Kill: An Examination of the Treatment of Juveniles Who Kill in Different European Countries*, Winchester: Waterside Press.

Comparative study based on papers delivered at an international conference focusing on the differing ways in which children who kill are dealt with by juvenile justice systems across Europe.

Christie, A. (1998) 'A comparison of arguments for employing men as child care workers and social workers in Denmark and the UK', *Social Work in Europe* 5(1): 2-17.

Draws on developments in child care services in Denmark and the UK to review arguments for and against including male social worker's employment in childcare services. These arguments exist within the overlapping domains of childcare and the labour market. Explores tensions between promoting equal opportunity objectives and pursuing the development of childcare services. Provides a profile of social work and child care workers in Denmark and the UK.

Christopherson, R. J. (1992-1993) 'The impact of children's helplines: an international comparison', *Practice* 6(4): 299-306.

Reports research that compared the impact of children's helplines in the UK, the Irish Republic and the Netherlands, and analyses the helplines' published statistics together with national population statistics and available prevalence studies.

Christopherson, R. J. (1998) 'Social work students' perceptions of child abuse: an international comparison and postmodern interpretation of its findings', *British Journal of Social Work* 28(1): 57-72.

Discusses how the decision about whether behaviour with children is acceptable has far reaching consequences for those involved. This articles aims to identify how far social work students achieve a consensus on the acceptability of behaviour, and whether similar items achieve agreement between groups in Sweden and England. Key findings are that there is little consensus within societies about what is acceptable behaviour towards children, Discusses the findings and makes recommendations for practice.

Cohen, B. and Hagen, U. (eds) (1997) *Children's Services: Shaping up for the Millennium; Supporting Children in the UK and Scandinavia*, Edinburgh: Stationery Office.

Comparative study exploring a wide range of services providing care, protection, education, health and recreation for children and young people in the United Kingdom and Scandinavia. This study focuses on three main themes central to the development of these services. Firstly, the response by those planning, providing or working in children's services to the growing emphasis on children's rights and ways of promoting involvement of children, young people and their parents or carers in the decision making process and in policy development. Secondly, structures and methods of working which foster inter-agency collaboration in service provision. Thirdly, finding ways in which services can be made more accountable to children, young people and their parents or carers.

Colton, M., Hellinckx, W., Bullock, R., and van den Bruel, B. (1991) 'Caring for troubled children in Flanders, the Netherlands and the United Kingdom', *British Journal of Social Work* 21(4): 381-392.

Reviews research on residential care and other services for disturbed children in Belgium and Holland and makes comparisons with services in the United Kingdom.

Colton, M.J. and Hellinckx, W. (eds) (1993) *Child Care in the EC: a Country Specific Guide to Foster and Residential Care* Aldershot: Arena.

Systematic description of policy, practice and research in residential child care and foster care in each of the EC member states, drawing on the experiences of EUSARF - the European Scientific Association on Residential and Foster Care for Children and Adolescents.

Colton, M. and Williams, M. (eds) (1997) *The World of Foster Care: an International Sourcebook on Foster Family Care Systems*, Aldershot: Arena.

Describes the role and structure of foster family care systems in 21 countries. Looks at: jurisdiction; history; origins; administration and organisation, foster children and parents; financial support for foster parents; problems and trends; role of the national foster parent organisation; and research.

Cooper, A. (1992) 'Anxiety and child protection work in two national systems', *Journal of Social Work Practice* 6(2): 117-128.

Examines how professional anxiety in child protection work can be understood as a function of the total system in which the work takes place, illustrated by research results from a comparative study of the French and English systems. All child protection work will mobilise powerful unconscious fantasy and anxiety in practitioners; but differences in the relationship between the social work and legal parts of the system in France and England serve as important factors in containing or perpetuating such anxiety.

Cooper, A. et al. (1992) *The social work role in child protection: an Anglo-French comparison. The report of a Pilot Study*, London: West London Institute of Higher Education/Association Jeunnesse Culture Loisirs Technique.

Reports on a pilot study which aimed to test and refine a methodology which enabled the comparison of structural, ideological and cultural dimensions of the French and English child protection systems in order to find not only equivalence but uniqueness as well. Includes a chapter on the French child protection system, with details of the roles played by various agencies (DISS - Directions des Interventions Sanitaires et Sociales, ASE - Aide Sociale a l'Enfance, PMI - Protection Maternelle et Infantile) and professionals (assistantes sociales of the DISS, Inspecteurs, educateurs specialises and psychologists of the ASE).

Cooper, A. (1994) 'In care or En Famille? Child protection, the family and the state in France and England', *Social Work in Europe* 1(1): 59-67.

Offers an analysis of contemporary English and French child protection social work in the light of recent research carried out by the West London Institute comparing the UK system and practices with those in France.

Cooper, A. (1994) 'A tale of two cultures - race, ideology and child protection work in France and England', *Social Work in Europe* 1(3): 53-60.

Analyses child protection work and interprets daily practice in

France and England, taking into account the separate historical, political and cultural contexts of the two nations.

Cooper, A., et al. (1995) *Positive child protection: a view from abroad,* Lyme Regis: Russell House.

Offers practitioners, administrators, and students a perspective on the French system of child protection, comparing it with the UK system and the Children Act 1989. Also presents models of French practice and supervision.

Cornia, G. A. and Sipos, S. (1991) *Children and the Transition to the Market Economy: Safety Nets and Social Policies in Central and Eastern Europe*, Aldershot: Avebury.

Cornick, J. C., Meyers, M. K. and Ross, K. E. (1997) 'Supporting the employment of mothers: policy variation across fourteen welfare estates', *Journal of European Social Policy* 7(1): 45-70.

This study compares OECD countries, as of the middle-to-late 1980s, with respect to the provision of policies that support mothers' employment: parental leave, child care, and the scheduling of public education. The empirical results reveal loose clusters of countries that correspond only partially to prevailing welfare typologies. For mothers with pre-school aged children, only five of the countries provided reasonably complete and continuous benefits that supported their options for combining paid work with family responsibilities. The pattern of cross-national policy variation changed notably when policies affecting mothers with older children were examined.

Crosby, I. (ed.) (1989): *'Love is not Enough', Conference Papers of the 5th international Foster Care Conference, Leeds*: Leeds Social Services Department.

A collection of conference papers on various aspects of foster care, child abuse, training, leaving care, mentally handicapped children, adult foster care, violence, recruitment of foster parents, long-term foster care.

Davies, M., and Sale, A. (1989) *Child Protection in Europe*, London: NSPCC.

Devore, W. and Seale, A. (1993) 'Ideas in action - an international social work curriculum for children and families - United Kingdom and United States perspectives', *Social Work Education* 12(2): 67.

This paper offers a comparison between the perspectives of the United Kingdom and United States in training and educating social workers, incorporating an historical overview.

Dioso, A. (1994) 'Learning from each other: professional Gypsy foster parents in Hungary', *Adoption and Fostering* 18(4): 38-42.

Throughout the Czech Republic, Slovakia, Hungary and Romania, a large ethnic minority group, generally known as 'Gypsies', has for generations suffered from discrimination and social ostracism. Discovers that the majority of children in state care are of Gypsy origin and reports on the tragedy, that these children have little chance of obtaining work on leaving care, and may not even be offered any care at all.

Edwards, S. M. and Soetenhorst de Savornin, L. (1994) 'The impact of "moral panic" on professional behaviour in cases of child sexual abuse: an international perspective', *Journal of Child Sexual Abuse* 3(1): 103-126.

Examines the narrative of two child abuse epidemics, one in Cleveland, England, the other in Vlaardingen, the Netherlands. The impact these incidents have had upon professionals is examined. The political reaction, and the media presentation adopted, provide another source of comparison. The media reports show a striking similarity in the condemnation of intervention from the judiciary and helping professions, and the concentration of the public debate on the method of diagnosis. On a theoretical level the analysis of the concept of Folk Devil, and the feminist perspective (the concept of Patriarch and Gender) allow for a transcultural approach, which takes into account the unequal power balances within the family in particular and society in general.

European Communities Commission: (1993) *Childcare in partnership: local authority/employer partnership initiatives in the European Community*, Brussels: Directorate General V. Employment, Industrial Relations and Social Affairs.

Report describing a range of partnership initiatives in the development of childcare services and other relevant work and family provisions in nine European Community countries.

Gilbert, N. (ed.) (1997) *Combating Child Abuse: International Perspectives and Trends*, Oxford: Oxford University Press.

Comparative study of the designs of child abuse reporting

operation of these systems and their outcomes and presents a viewpoint on policy options designed to protect children. Countries looked at are: United States; Canada; United Kingdom; Sweden; Denmark; Finland; Belgium; Netherlands; and Germany.

Gottesmann, M. (ed.) (1991) *Residential Child Care: An International Reader*, London: Whiting and Birch/Social Care Association.

Chapters on Austria, Belgium, Canada, Czechoslovakia, Denmark, FRG, GDR, Finland, France, Great Britain, Hungary, Ireland, Israel, Italy, Yugoslavia (Slovenia and Croatia), Luxembourg, Netherlands, Poland, Sweden, Switzerland, USA.

Gottesmann, M. (ed.) (1994) *Recent Changes and New Trends in Extrafamilial Child Care: An International Perspective*, London: Whiting and Birch.

Looks at recent changes and trends in child care world-wide and presents a range of case studies to demonstrate new and radical approaches to child care outside the family, looking particularly at residential child and youth care.

Hantrais, L. (1994) 'Family policy in Europe' in Page, R. and Baldock, J., *Social Policy Review 6*, Social Policy Association.

Hantrais, L. and Letablier, M -T. (eds) (1996) *Comparing Families and Family Policies in Europe*, Loughborough: Loughborough University.

Includes chapters on: comparing families and family policies in Europe; statistics for comparing new family forms; lesbian families in the UK and France; researching family obligations; non-take-up of benefits in France; family sociology and ideology in Spain; sociological perspectives on the family-employment relationship in France; women's employment and equal opportunities; the relationship between women's paid and unpaid work; combining care and paid employment; changing gender roles and family-employment strategies in Spain; policies for employed mothers in France and Italy; and constructing categories for comparing family policy making.

Hazekamp, J. L. and Popple, K. (eds) (1997) *Racism in Europe: a Challenge for Youth Policy and Youth Work*, London: UCL Press.

Examines the rise of racism in Europe and its impact on young people. Covers Belgium, Germany, the Netherlands, Spain and the United Kingdom. Examines and compares existing strategies and policies affecting young people and considers the future and policies affecting young people and considers the future development of appropriate youth policy and youth work practice.

Hellinckx W., Colton, M. and Williams M. (eds) (1997) *International Perspectives on Family Support*, Aldershot: Arena.

Provides an overview of family preservation services which integrates theory, policy and practice both within various programmes and between different countries in Europe and North America. Part 1 provides a general outline in which authors discuss theoretical aspects of child-rearing, the causes and characteristics of problems which can arise and the kind of service best suited to particular situations. Part 2 contains more practice-oriented material through the exploration of case studies and individual programmes. Part 3 focuses on the evaluation of family support.

Herczog, M. (1998) 'Assessing child welfare outcomes in Central and Eastern Europe', *Children and Society* 12 (2): 223-227.

Hetherington, R. and Pitts, J. (eds) (1992) *Protecting children in Europe: papers from the first symposium on perspectives on European child care,* London: West London Institute, Department of Social Work.

Papers from a conference which covered: a French perspective on child protection in England; and English perspective on child protection in France; the system in Scotland; the challenges in the establishment of a new child protection system in Poland; and observations on international comparative research.

Hooper-Brair, K. and Lawson, H.A. (1995) 'Families and social development. New global development', *Journal of International and Comparative Social Welfare* 11(1): 1-14.

Only rarely have families and their well-being served as a cornerstone for social development policies and practices. Supportive and effective social development for families will build upon their identifiable needs, challenges, strengths, and capacities, involving them as partners. Once the focus is upon families, social development initiatives aimed at full rewarding employment; the reduction and eradication of poverty, the support of caregivers must become integrated. Families may guide and deliver services and supports, playing key roles in mutual aid networks. In substitution for categorical policies and practices, a relational, family centred approach promotes family well-being at the same time it facilitates social development.

Hudson, J. and Galaway, B. (eds) (1989) *The state as parent: international research perspectives on interventions with young persons* Dordrecht, Netherlands: Kluwer.

Edited papers from a research workshop, 'State Intervention on Behalf of Children and Youth', held in Maratea, Italy, 20-24 February 1989. Divided into 4 sections: organisation and accountability for state intervention; young persons in conflict with the law; child abuse; and children in care.

Ingerslev, H. (1999) 'Aspects of decision-making systems concerning compulsory child protection measures in the Netherlands, Denmark and Norway', *Social Work in Europe* 6(1): 30-40.

This article compares elements of the decision-making procedures in compulsory child protection measures in the Netherlands, Denmark and Norway.

Jarvis, S. and Redmond, G. (1997) 'Welfare state regimes and child poverty in the UK and Hungary', *Journal of European Social Policy* 7(4): 275-290.

Describes how recent social policy reforms in Hungary have signalled a significant reduction in state support for working mothers, including the introduction of means-tested benefits for families with children. This article argues that this represents a move towards a welfare-state regime similar to that found in the UK, which, for families with children, encourages the 'breadwinner' household where the father is the sole earner and the mother works in the home. Maintains that the reforms recently implemented in Hungary can be expected to lead to increases in child poverty, the incidence of which is partly determined by the degree of welfare state support for families with children and the extent of female participation in the labour market.

Korintus, M. (1994) 'Childcare in Hungary', *Concern* 88 (Spring): 4-5.

Looks at the childcare system for children under three in Hungary. State support for mothers is relatively generous, however, the economic situation is driving more women into full-time employment. At the same time, the cost of providing childcare is an enormous burden on the state budget. The 1992 Social Act passed many of the state's responsibilities on to local authorities. The National Institute of Day Care Centres (BOMI) are working to make available a wider range of childcare services and to provide training and guidelines for services.

Lamonby, S. (1996) 'The international initiative: children youth families - a new approach', *Social Work in Europe* 3(1): 30-32.

Looks at the evolution, aims and forthcoming priorities of the international organisation 'The International Initiative' which was established in January 1992. Professionals involved in the group include policy makers, managers, researchers and practitioners. Their aim is to find new approaches to strengthen and support children, youth and families.

Luckock, B. Volger, R. and Keating, H. (1997) 'The Belgian Flemish child protection system: confidentiality, voluntarism and coercion', *Child and Family Law Quarterly* 9(2): 101-113.

Discusses how debates over the child protection system in the UK have been enlivened by comparative analysis of continental procedure. In particular, enthusiastic claims have been made about the approaches adopted in both France and Belgium. Both systems, so it is claimed, avoid the legalism and the punitive attitudes of the English and Welsh system, thus making child protection more effective for children and families and less antagonistic and demoralising for child care professionals. Describes a comparative pilot study of the role of judicial decision making in France, in the Flemish Community in Belgium, and in England.

Madge, N. (1994) *Children and residential care in Europe* London: National Children's Bureau, European Children's Centre.

Looks broadly at children and child care services, especially residential child care, in the 12 European Union countries and Sweden, to give an overview of national similarities and differences and identify key areas of change, development and concern.

Myers, S. (1998) 'Young people who sexually abuse: is consensus possible or desirable?', *Social Work in Europe* 5(1): 53-56.

Compares approaches to the problem of young people who sexually abuse in Europe with the situation in the USA.

Ray, J.C. (1997) 'The role of demographic and economic characteristics of twelve member states of the European Union in the diversity of state support for families', *Journal of European Social Policy* 7(1): 5-16.

This study is based upon an international data set comprising state support for families in fifteen countries. Using multiple regression analysis, the levels of state support are explained by the principle parameters used for setting levels of benefit, and by the demographic and economic characteristics of the countries concerned.

Ruxton, S. (1997) 'Children in Europe - policies and prospects', *Social Work in Europe* 4(1): 17-23.

Describes available statistics and research about the about the position of children in the Member States of the European Union today. Aims to indicate the current and future impact on children of economic, social and demographic change; and to draw up recommendations for the development of legislation, policy and services.

Selman, P. (1993) 'Services for intercountry adoption in the UK : some lessons from Europe', *Adoption and Fostering*, 17(3): 14-19.

What should a comprehensive UK policy on intercountry adoption consist of? Considers some of the lessons to be learnt from the Netherlands and Sweden.

Sinclair, R. (1989) *Child care in Norway and England. A useful comparison?* Leicester: Leicestershire Social Services Department.

Reports the findings from a study trip to Norway under the auspices of the Council of Europe.

Slukin, A. and Dolan, P. (1990) 'Tackling child abuse in the European Community', *Journal of Social Work Practice* 4(2): 98-102.

It is increasingly realised that child abuse exists in all societies. Finkelhor (1988), in a seminal paper, suggests that the main focus of international concern should be 'parental battering, selective neglect and sexual abuse'. Discussion of the climate of opinion and the procedures adopted to protect children in three EC countries: the Netherlands, France and West Germany.

Smith, P. (1995) 'Subsidiarity and the role of the social worker in Germany and England', *Social Work in Europe* 2(3): 54-56.

Discusses the results of a joint research project undertaken by Brunel University College and the Fachhochschule of Rheinland Pfalz in Koblenz comparing the German and English child protection systems. Social workers from each country were given a case study and then discussed how they would handle the case. The article focuses on the concept of subsidiarity in particular and how it is understood in German and English social work. Gives both English and German views of the working methods of their overseas colleagues.

Thomas, T. (1998) 'The CUPICSO Project - protecting children across Europe', *Social Work in Europe* 5(3): 58.

CUPISCO stands for Collection and Use of Personal Information on Child Sex Offenders. The use of personal information is seen to have moved to centre stage in the policing of sex offenders and the aim here was to examine the databases kept by the EU Member States on information relating to known and convicted abusers. Having identified who was holding these databases, the CUPISCO Project went on to look at how this information was being used.

Van Wormer, K. (1993) 'Child welfare practice in cultural context: Norway and the USA', *International Social Work* 36(4): 301-314.

Social work focus and behaviour may seem strange to the outside observer if not understood within the cultural context. This paper attempts to show that values central to Norwegian life - egalitarianism, trust in authority, and reliance on the government to solve individual problems - shape social work activity to a degree that overrides professional theory and knowledge. The arena of child welfare is examined in terms of professional image, prestige and power.

Warman, A. (1998) 'Family obligations in Europe: an exploration of family / state boundaries', *Social Work in Europe* 5(2): 48-55.

Describes research which examined the family / state boundaries in Europe and in particular, to look at whether these boundaries were shifting in response to changes in the work force and demographic factors.

Weightman, K. and Weightman, A. (1995) '"Never right, never wrong": child welfare and social work in England and Sweden', *Scandinavian Journal of Social Welfare* 4(2): 75-84.

When are parents 'unfit' to care for their own children? As in many other countries, social workers in England and Sweden have the unenviable task of forming such judgements. On behalf of society at large, social workers must balance the rights of parents to provide continuing care with the responsibilities of the state in ensuring adequate care of children. In both England and Sweden, social workers are able to seek legal orders which, if granted, permit compulsory removal of children against the wishes of parents. In such cases, social workers are centrally involved in processes which remove ordinary rights of citizenship from their fellow members of society. The rights of parents and children, together with the responsibilities of the state to each class of citizen, are clearly in focus: intervention in family life requires both grounds and legitimation. But what is the basis for intervention in the two societies? Social work practices in Sweden and England suggest very different answers to this question. In explaining the differences, it is necessary to address much broader variations of social and political culture in the two societies. In so doing, variations in social work practice can be located in different cultural values and systems of legitimation. Instabilities and pathologies of professional practices can also be identified within both England and Sweden.

Wilford, G. (1997) 'One story - different perspectives: users of child care services in England and Germany', *Social Work in Europe* 4(1): 23-31.

A comparative survey of families in England, France and Germany of their impressions and opinions of the treatment they received when they needed either help bringing up children, or when official social services intervened.

Wiman, R. (1994) *On the rights of children with special needs in changing Europe*, Helsinki: National Research and Development Centre for Welfare and Health.

Windebank, J. (1996) 'To what extent can social policy challenge the dominant ideology of mothering? A cross-national comparison of Sweden, France and Britain', *Journal of European Social Policy* 6(2): 147-161.

The question of who looks after children is a function of the social construction of 'mothering'. Although the exact nature and distribution of 'mothering' work changes according to the cultural and historical context, mothering has remained inextricably linked to gender. Indeed, numerous studies have shown that fathers' involvement in child care has not increased to match mother's involvement in the labour force and that women remain the principal carers for children. The aim of this article is to provide a systematic study of the ways in which different welfare regimes may have helped challenge the dominant ideology of mothering by fostering a distribution of child care which assists mothers in their employment and which gives child care providers social and economic status. This is achieved by investing in mothers' employment patterns, policies towards parenting and child care, child care practices and the status of child care providers in Sweden, France and Britain. The finding is that in all three welfare regimes, the ability of some mothers even partially to deconstruct their 'mothering' role relies on the existence of other women who are not in such an advantageous position, to act as 'mother substitutes'. It is concluded that social policies which do not address the issue of fathers' roles in providing the flexibility necessary to reconcile child care and parental employment will result in a 'zero sum game' for women as a group vis-à-vis their caring duties.

Disability (physical and learning)

Aarts, L. J. M., Burkhauser R. V., and De Jong P. R. (eds) (1996) *Curing the Dutch Disease: An International Perspective on Disability Policy Reform,* Aldershot: Avebury.

Comparative study evaluating Dutch disability policies from the 1970s onwards. Experts from Germany, Sweden, the United Kingdom and the United States go on to use the evaluation framework to compare policies in their own countries.

George, M. (1991) 'Disability in Europe', *Community Care* 882: 26-7.

Advocacy has emerged as a key concept in the process of the modernisation of western psychiatry. This article combines a general discussion of the advocacy approach with an analysis of its application in practice. Two projects which are among the most advanced projects of professional advocacy in European mental health are used for discussion.

Grana, J.M. (1983) 'Disability allowances for long-term care in Western Europe and the United States', *International Social Security Review* 36(2): 207-21.

This article explores the implications of the efficient provision of non-institutional long-term care services, such as personal care and social services. The relative efficiency of cash versus restricted transfers is discussed, with special emphasis on disability allowances for long-term care. Cash allowances programmes in five European nations and in the United States Veterans Administration are analysed, based on reports and legislation and on the author's personal interviews with the ministries concerned with social insurance, social assistance, and veterans. Conclusions about disability allowances for long-term care and their potential as a reform option for long-term care are formulated.

Hutten, J. B.F. and Kerkstra A. (eds) (1996) *Home Care in Europe: A Country-Specific Guide to its Organisation and Financing*, Aldershot: Arena

Comparative study of the organisation and financing of home care in the 15 member states of the European Union. Defines home care as nursing care at home and home help services.

Ruppel, F. and King, A. (1995) 'German care insurance and British community care: comparative perspectives', *Social Work in Europe* 2(1): 12-17.

Considers the recently enacted German care insurance scheme - 'Pflegeversicherung', which provides the legislative and financial framework for the care of chronically sick and disabled people. The emphasis in provision is now on expanding the infrastructure of non-residential, home and community-based provision and on allowing persons in need of care to remain in a domiciliary environment.

Mental health

Appleby, L. and Araya, R. (eds) (1991) *Mental Health Services in the Global Village*, London: Gaskell.

Comparative study of mental health services in 16 countries from both the developed and the developing world. Contains sections on countries from Asia, Europe, Africa, the Middle East and South and Central America.

Brandon, D. et al. (1998) 'European snap-shot survey of attitudes towards mental health', *Breakthrough* 2(2): 5-20.

Presents the results of a survey covering 8 European cities in the countries of: Switzerland, England, Ukraine, Portugal, Russia, Sweden, Italy and Croatia which looks at people attitudes and contact with mental health problems.

Challis, D., Davies, B., and Traske, K (eds) (1994) *Community Care: New Agendas and Challenges from the UK and Overseas*, Aldershot: Arena.

Dickey, B. and Scott, J. (1997) 'An international comparison of cost and outcomes of psychiatric care: research and policy implications', *Journal of Mental Health* 6(3): 251-263.

This article compares two clinical services for the seriously mentally ill in two catchment areas, one in the US and one in the UK, with similar demography. In addition, the study identifies methodological challenges to the conduct of international health services research. A random sample of vulnerable individuals with severe and enduring mental illnesses, treated in the community, was compared on clinical observation and self-reported ratings of health status. Patterns of care and treatment cost were analysed prospectively over a 12-month period.

Forster, R. (1998) 'Patient advocacy in psychiatry: the Austrian and Dutch models', *International Social Work* 41(2): 155-168.

Goodwin, S. (1997) *Comparative Mental Health Policy: From Institutional to Community Care*, London: Sage.

Comparative analysis of mental health policy in Western Europe and North America. This book considers how, and why, differences have developed in the implementation of these policies. Examines the transition from institutional to community based models of care; identifies variations in the inception, pace and style in which community based service provision has emerged in different countries; assesses the problems and issues that have arisen as a result of the shift towards community care and treatment; and argues that it is a policy made up of conflicting aims and purposes and that this is reflected in its implementation.

Jones, K. (1988) *Experience in Mental Health: Community Care and Social Policy,* London: Sage.

Presents a broad comparison of detailed research into the policies and experiences of community mental health in four countries - the USA, UK, Italy and China.

Korr, W.S. (1993) 'The UN convention on the rights of the child: Implications for mental health policy' in Ekberg, K. and Mjaavatn P. E. *Children at Risk: Proceedings*, Trodenheim: The Norwegian Centre for Child Research.

Peltonen-Heikinenen, R. (1995) 'Scandinavian style of care', *Nursing Times*, 17 May: 40-41.

Reports from Finland on comparisons which can be made with mental health services in the UK.

Savio, M. (1996) 'Community care and inter-professional relationships: Community psychiatric nursing in Britain and Italy', Social *Work in Europe* 3(3): 1-11

This paper focuses on comparative analysis of community

psychiatric nursing in Britain and Italy and explores some of the differences in the division of labour between the psychiatric nurses (CPNs) and Social Workers (SWs) in the two countries. A multiple case study research approach has been used to examine cross-nationally the growth and development of community psychiatric nursing in Britain and Italy. The study aimed at achieving the following objectives: (1) to provide a documented comparison between the professional experience of British and Italian CPNs interviewed; (2) to investigate similarities and differences between community psychiatric nursing practices in the two countries in relation to organisational models, ideological approaches to care, and professional cultures; and (3) to propose a tentative theory about the growth and development of community psychiatric nursing as a cross-national endeavour.

Taylor, R. (1997) 'International perspectives on British mental health services', *Social Work Education* 16(3): 5-20.

This paper illustrates the importance of providing international perspectives on key areas of mental health policy and practice for students undergoing social work education and training. As part of a three year BA Social Work Studies degree at the Manchester Metropolitan University the final year teaching which follows on from students' professional qualification includes electives which provide international perspectives on a range of social work issues. One of these electives is a study of international perspectives in mental health. The central themes which emerge from this comparative study are the need to counter the individualising of mental distress and the limited part which case management currently plays in this process.

Wilder, J. (1997) 'Surmounting frontiers: mental illness and rehabilitation', *Social Work in Europe* 4(2): 33-35.

Describes some of the activities of members of the Helios programme which has funded seminars in various countries to explore and share ideas which might enable better lives for disabled people.

Offenders

Allen, R. (1993) 'Responding to youth crime in Norway: suggestions for England and Wales', *Howard Journal* 32(2): 99-113.

This paper describes and compares recent development in youth justice in Norway with those in England and Wales. in particular measures proposed or undertaken with severely persistent juvenile offenders. The paper offers explanations of recent changes in policy and practice.

Downes, D. (1994) 'Serious diversions: juvenile crime and justice in Europe and the lessons for Britain', *Social Work in Europe* 1(2): 4-12.

Argues the need for comparative study of crime and its control, reviews juvenile justice in England and Wales over the past two decades, considers the need for diversion to be taken seriously, the wider context, and the politics of law and order.

Gibson, P. (1994) 'Towards a European definition of persistency', *Social Work in Europe* 1(2): 54-61.

Looks at the nature of persistency in relation to young offenders, the need for a European definition or understanding of persistency, citizenship as a way forward for practice, and a framework for policy and practice which is based on social integration.

Haines, J. (1995) 'Intensive supervision', *Social Work in Europe* 2(1): 45-7

Reports on a CEP (Permanent European Conference on Probation and After Care) seminar on intensive supervision held in Oslo in September 1994.

Pitts, J. (1994) 'What can we learn in Europe?', *Social Work in Europe* 1(1): 48-54.

Pitts, J. (1997) 'Crime, justice and social exclusion in Europe', *Social Work in Europe* 4(3): 11-13.

The concern about 'social exclusion' is inextricably tied up with concern about crime. Opinion polls confirm that a large majority of European citizens are worried about crime per se, and the prospect of violent victimisation in particular. Many believe that the major threat comes from those who inhabit the social and economic margin. In the 1980s and 1990s, these fears have often been exploited by politicians seeking re-election. That the volume of crime is rising is indisputable; that this rise is simply attributable to crime from the social margins is, at least, unlikely.

Pitts, J. (1997) 'Restorative justice: a better deal for the socially excluded', *Social Work in Europe* 4(3): 49-57.

In May 1997, at a conference in Belgium, penal reformers and academics from Europe, North America and Australasia put their signatures to the *Declaration of Leuven*. In this document, they affirmed their belief that 'restorative justice' was superior in every respect to existing systems of retributive justice. The Declaration of Leuven has been dismissed by some critics as the utopian outpouring of a handful of politically marginal intellectuals and would-be social reformers. However, this ignores the reality that, in the recent period, youth justice systems in many European states and other advanced anglophone nations around the world have introduced substantial elements of restorative justice.

Whitfield, D. (1997) 'Tagging: the European contexts and comparisons', *Social Work in Europe* 4(3): 43-48.

Looks at what can be learnt from the European experience of tagging offenders.

Older people

Age Concern England (1997) *Who cares for an ageing Europe: a report by the European Resource Unit at Age Concern England*, London: Age Concern England.

This is a brief report on the major challenge facing European countries as the proportion of older Europeans grows. The report offers a brief overview of care for older people across Europe, comparing the situations in different member states as well as making general points about the whole of the European Union.

Anderson, R. (1992) *The Coming of Age in Europe: Older People in the European Community*, Age Concern, England.

Crosby, G., (ed.), et al. (1993) *The European directory of older age: information and organisations concerned with older people in the 12 EC member states*, London: Centre for Policy on Ageing.

Daatland, S.O. (1997) 'Welfare policies for older people in transition? Emerging trends and comparative perspectives', *Scandinavian Journal of Social Welfare* 6(3): 153-161.

This article examines how three Scandinavian countries are responding to the seemingly growing gap between demands and resources. Various strategies and approaches are identified and evaluated, and their relevance and potential are discussed in a comparative context across time and between countries.

Davies, L. (ed.) (1992) *The Coming of Age in Europe: Older People in the European Community*, London: Age Concern England.

This is a comparative study of provision for older people in the European Community. It identifies trends and highlights good practice in a variety of fields, including employment and retirement, pensions and benefits, housing, transport, leisure and health care. Uses case studies as illustrations.

Eales, R. (1990) 'Here today, gone tomorrow: the vanishing generation', *Lloyds Log*, June: 48-49.

Discusses the changing population patterns in Europe and the effect on employment and insurance.

Evers, A., and Svetlik, I. (1991) *New Welfare Mixes in Care for the Elderly. Volume 2: Austria, Denmark, Finland, Israel, Netherlands (Eurosocial Report 40/2)*, Vienna: European Centre Social Welfare Policy & Research

Chapter 1. Christoph Badelt and Jan Pazourek, Care for the Older People in Austria. Chapter 2. Peter Abrahamson, Welfare for older people in Denmark: from institutionalisation to self-reliance? Chapter 3. Anneli Anttonen, Care for older people in Finland and the future of the Scandinavian caring state. Chapter 4. Arnold M. Gross, Israel. Chapter 5. Netherlands, Marja A. Pijl.

Evers, A., Leichsenring, and K. (1994) 'Paying for informal care - an issue of growing importance', *Ageing International*, 21(1): 29-40.

Considers developments in Europe, with specific reference to Belgium, Finland, Sweden, the Netherlands, and Austria.

Giarchi, G.G. (1996) *Caring for older Europeans: Comparative Studies in 29 Countries*, Aldershot: Arena.

Provides a reference source for various modes of care (both formal and informal) for older people throughout Europe. Each chapter includes: demography; socio-political and administrative background; social security and pensions; housing; health care; mental health care; residential care; personal social services; voluntary care agencies and support organisations; leisure pursuits and education; and older people in rural areas.

Gillion, C. (1991) 'Ageing populations: spreading the costs', *Journal of European Social Policy* 1(2): 107-28.

Gillion discusses the international implications of an increasing ageing population and the burden this phenomenon is placing on social security and taxation.

Glendinning, C. (ed.) (1998) *Rights and Realities,* Bristol: The Policy Press.

All major industrial societies are experiencing changing demographic profiles, with numbers of very elderly people likely to peak over the next four decades. These demographic changes are accompanied by political pressures to limit increases in public expenditure. This text examines such issues from the perspectives of several countries that have recently made changes to the organisation, funding or delivery of health and social welfare services for frail elderly people. These are: UK, Germany, Netherlands, Finland, Denmark, and Australia.

Glendinning, C., and Mclaughlin, E. (1993) 'Paying for informal care: lessons from Finland', *Journal of European Social Policy*, 3(4): 239-253.

Growing numbers of older people, combined with falling birth-rates, have generated increased interest within most western European and Scandinavian countries in measures which might increase the supply of care-giving labour while at the same time reducing the unit costs of that labour, and the extent to which expensive formal service provision can be replaced by less costly and more plentiful help from informal sources. Describes the pressures for change in the UK, especially the shortcomings in the current social security approach to paying informal care-givers; the demands of disabled people for greater control over personal assistance services; and the implementation of the community care reforms. It then describes and evaluates the Finnish system of Home Care Allowances, in which local municipalities pay friends and relatives who are providing a very substantial amount of care to a frail elderly person.

Guillemard, A. M. (1991) 'The decline of social status? Evolution of the welfare state for the elderly in Europe - the past situation and future prospects' in Pacolet, J. and Wilderom, C. *The Economics of Care of the Elderly*, Avebury: Aldershot.

Jakobsson, G. (1998) 'The politics of care for elderly people in Scandinavia', *European Journal of Social Work* 1(1): 87-93.

Describes the issues currently impacting on the social welfare system in Scandinavia, especially as they affect older people.

Jamieson, A., and Illsley, R. (eds) (1990) *Contrasting European Policies for the Care of the Elderly*, London: Avebury.

Looks at Belgium, Denmark, France, Greece, Germany, Ireland, Italy, the Netherlands, and the UK. Part 1 examines the relationship between formal and informal care; Part 2 deals with care systems and care delivery problems.

Jamieson, A. (1991) 'Community care for older people: policies in Britain, West Germany and Denmark' in Room, G. (ed.) *Towards a European Welfare State*, Bristol: SAUS Publications.

Jamieson, A. (1992) 'Home care in old age: a lost cause?', *Journal of Health Politics, Policy and Law* 17(4): 879-898.

Considers policy trends and the provision of home care for frail older people in four countries: Denmark, the United Kingdom, Germany and the United States. The differing nature of health and social service systems of each country and the welfare ideologies that underlie them have affected the expansion of home care for this group of people. Hence, Denmark - and to a lesser extent Britain - has relatively well developed networks of home care services, in contrast to Germany and the United States. However, any significant shift away from predominantly medical and institutional care to more home-based, social care is highly unlikely.

Jamieson, A. (ed.) (1991) *Home Care for Older People in Europe: Policies and Practices,* Oxford: Oxford University Press.

Keighler, S. (1990) *'Compensating Relatives Who Care for Elderly Kin: Policy Foundations in Two Neo-Conservative Social Welfare States'*, Paper presented at the British Social Policy Association Annual Meeting, July, Bath.

Kraan, R. J. et al (eds) (1991) *Care for the Elderly. Significant Innovations in Three European Countries*, Frankfurt am Main: Campus

Litwin, H. and Lightman, E. (1996) 'The development of community care policy for the elderly: A comparative perspective', *International Journal of Health Services* 26(4): 691-708.

Maddox, G. L. (1992) 'Long-term care policies in comparative perspective', *Ageing and Society* 12(3): 355-368.

Outlines long term care policies in the United States and the variety of approaches within the European union.

McDerment, L., and Greengross, S. (1985) *Social Care for Elderly People: An International Perspective*, Surbiton: Social Care Association.

Introduces some of the major issues in residential care for older people in an international framework through the use of descriptive case material. Includes articles on residential for the elderly in: Germany, Japan, Denmark, South Africa, Liberia, Sweden and the United States of America.

Nies, H., Tester, S. and Nuijens, J. M. (1991) 'Day care in the United Kingdom and the Netherlands: a comparative study', *Ageing and Society* 11(3): 245-273.

Compares social policy and legislation, service delivery, types of service and user characteristics, and discusses issues of policy and practice.

Organisation for Economic Co-operation and Development (1988) *Ageing Population: the Social Policy Implications*, Paris: OECD.

Overbye, E. (1997) 'Mainstream pattern, deviant cases: the New Zealand and Danish pension systems in an international context', *Journal of European Social Policy* 7(2): 101-117.

In the late 19th and early 20th century, industrialised countries introduced a variety of pension schemes to sustain older people. These initial schemes may broadly be classified as 'contributory' or 'assisted' by women working in three European countries: Italy, Germany and England. This article examines the extent to which factors such as women's roles, caring and gender difference impacted upon work styles, practice and management in social work and on policy development in the personal social services.

Pacolet, J. and Wilderom, C. (eds) (1991) *The Economics of Care of the Elderly*, Avebury: Aldershot.

Pampel, F. C. (1992) 'Trends in living alone among the elderly in Europe' in Rogers, A. *Elderly Migration and Population Redistribution - a Comparative Study*, Belhaven Press: London.

Rollet, C. (1991) 'Care for elderly people in the European Community'. *Social Policy and Administration* 25(3): 184-192.

All EEC countries are faced with an ageing population, which means an increase of people in some way handicapped in everyday activities. A comparison of the solutions adopted by several EEC countries in the sectors of housing, home care services, residential and nursing homes shows that a real medico-social policy has been worked out only in Denmark and the Netherlands. In France and the United Kingdom, public authorities have certainly defined policies that lay claim to providing overall coverage but they have not provided corresponding resources. In Germany and Italy, there is no clearly defined policy. This paper discusses the various factors, which may account for these differences.

Scott, P. and Johnson, P. (1988) *The Economic Consequences of Population Ageing in Advanced Societies*, London: Centre for Economic Policy Research.

Sipila, J. (1994) 'Why do the Scandinavian governments compensate family members who care for elderly kin?' *Care in Place: The International Journal of Networks and Community*, 1(3): 261-271.

Includes a commentary from Finland about government policy on financial compensation for carers. Current practices in Nordic countries are reviewed, with a brief overview of other European government policies, including the UK. Implications for health/social services staff, non- government workers, and carers are identified.

Teicher, M. I., Thursz, D., and Vigilante, J. L., (eds) (1979) *Reaching the Aged: Social Services in Forty-Four Countries*, London: Sage.

Volume 4 of the 'Social Service Delivery Systems - An International Annual' series. Commences with an international perspective on services for the aged, then looks at innovations in Israel and the U.S.A., then services for the aged in China, Italy, India and Poland, services for the aged sick in the U.S.A., Canada, Netherlands, Denmark, Norway, France and Belgium, and comparative overview of services in developed and developing countries, and comparative perspectives on services in Yugoslavia, Japan, Denmark, the Federal Republic of Germany, and South Africa.

Tinker, A. (1993) *Elderly People in Modern Society,* London: Longman.

Walker, A., Guillemard, A-M. and Alber, J. (1993) *Older People in Europe: Social and Economic Policies (The 1993 Report of the European Community Observatory)* Brussels, Commission of the European Communities.

Social work education

Aymer, C. and Bryan, A. (1998) 'Investigating inter-cultural communication within and between a British and Dutch social work course', *Social Work in Europe* 5(2): 59-65.

This article arises from an experiment that attempted to explore the following questions. What are the similarities and the differences in the way that cultural divisions are negotiated on a Dutch and a British social work programme? In comparing the two situations, how can a racially mixed British group of students think about the ways in which they communicated across cultures?

Barr, H. (1989) *Social Work in its European Context* London: Central Council for Education and Training in Social Work.

Barr, H. (1990) 'Measuring up to the EC directive', *Issues in Social Work Education* 10(1and2): 128-34.

This paper discusses the possible problems arising from the exclusion of social work in the UK from being covered by the European Commission (EC) Directive on Higher Education Diplomas. Social work in the UK might be subject to a second directive for lower level professions, thus formalising its inferior status. So what should happen now?

Barr, H. (1990) *Social Work Education and 1992 (In Europe 1)*, London: Central Council for Education and Training in Social Work.

Barr, H. (1989) *Social Work Education in its European Context*, London: Central Council for Education and Training in Social Work.

Blonden, F. (1991) 'Social work education for European mobility. Is a European professional profile possible?', *Issues in Social Work Education* 11(1): 85-91.

This paper poses a question 'Is there a common profile of professional social work practice across Europe?' The views of Landelijke Vereniging van Maatschappelijk Werkers (LVMW), the Netherlands Association of Social Workers are discussed.

Bogo, M., and Herington, W. (1988) 'Consultation in social work education in the international context', *International Social Work* 31(4): 304-16.

Bradley, G. and Firth, R. (1998) 'Translating the European dimension into training', *Social Work in Europe* 5(1): 49-53.

Looks at the way the European dimension is being transcribed within different social work education programmes in the UK.

Brauns, H-J. and Kramer, D. (1986) *Social Work Education in Europe. A Comprehensive Description of Social Work Education in 21 European Countries,* Frankfurt: Deutcher Verein für öffentliche und private Fürsorge.

Brown, K. (1994) 'A framework of teaching comparative social work' in Gehrmann, G., Muller, K.D., and Ploem, R. (eds) *Social Work and Social Work Studies: Co-operation in Europe 2000,* Weinheim: Deutcher Studien Verlag.

Cannan, C., Coleman, R., and Lyons, K. (1992) *Links and Exchanges (In Europe 2),* London: Central Council for Education and Training in Social Work.

CCETSW (1988) *Report from the European Directive Workshop*, London: Central Council for Education and Training in Social Work.

Chytil, O. and Seibel, F. (eds) (1999) *Eurpean Dimensions in Training and Practice in Social Professions* , Boskovice: ALBERT.

Cocozza, L. (1989) *Social Work Training in the European Community*, Luxembourg: Office for Official Publications of the European Community.

Cocozza, L. (ed.) (1990) *Social Workers in the European Community: Training-Employment- Perspectives* 1992, Report of La Hulpe Seminar: International Federation of Social Workers, La Hulpe, Belgium.

Commission of the European Communities (1990) *ECTS European Community Course Credit Transfer System,* Brussels: ERASMUS Bureau.

Commission of the European Communities (1989) 'Proposal for a council directive on a second general system for the recognition of professional education and training which compliments directive'. (89/48/EEC), *Official Journal of the European Communities* (October 16), C263/1

Constable, R., Mehta, V. (eds) (1994) *Education for Social Work in Eastern Europe: Changing Horizons,* Chicago, IL.: Lyceum Books/International Association of Schools of Social Work.

Chapter 1: From the culture of silence to the culture of freedom:

new directions in the practice of social work in Romania. Chapter 2: The context for practice and education in Polish social work: foundations for the international consultation process. Chapter 3: Social work practice and social work education in the Czech Republic. Chapter 4: Social work and social work education in Croatia. Chapter 5: Changing horizons of education in social work and human services in Hungary. Chapter 6: The emergence of social work in Lithuania. Chapter 7: The emergence of the profession of social work in the Russian Republic. Chapter 8: Common themes in curriculum development in social work education and the process of technical assistance.

Council of the European Communities (1989) 'Council directive of 21 December 1998 on a general system for the recognition of higher education diplomas awarded on completion of professional education and training of at least 3 Years duration' (89/48/EEC), *Official Journal of the European Communities* (9 January 24), L19/16

Cox, D. (1995) 'Social work education: state of the art', *Scandinavian Journal of Social Welfare* 4(3): 280-289

David Cox (1995) argues that social work educators need to engage with social issues if they are to move social work away from the doldrums in which it has become trapped. Although this is true, changes of a greater magnitude are required if social work practice is to remain relevant in the twenty-first century. In a globalizing world, social work educators have to play a key role in internationalising the social work curricula (academic and practicum) and socialising practitioners to embrace emancipatory approaches to social work if they are to counteract the brutalising forces of industrialism and militarism. Engaging with social change to empower excluded groups requires social workers to work with 'clients', policy makers and international welfare organisations in ways that link the personal and structural dimensions of social life. In short, practitioners need to go beyond the state of the art if their interventions are to respond to the 'person-in-their-situation' in a modern context.

Daines, R. (1992) *Bridging the Channel: Practice Teaching in France and the United Kingdom. Report of a Study Visit to Angers London*: Central Council for Education and Training in Social Work.

Reports on a visit to the Ecole Normale Sociale de l'Ouest at Angers by a group of practice teachers and a training officer from Avon and Gloucestershire SSDs to study practice teaching in

France. Gives an overview of practice in France and considers differences and similarities between the French and the U.K. practice, and outlines issues which may arise in future exchange.

Dalichow F., and Teichler, U. (1986) *Higher Education in the European Community: Recognition of Study Abroad in the European Community: the Findings of a Survey of Joint Study Programmes,* Brussels: Commission of the European Communities.

Doel, M. and Shardlow, S. M. (1996) *Social Work in a Changing World: an International Perspective on Practice*, Aldershot: Arena.

Estes, R.J. (1992) *Internationalising Social Work Education: A Guide to Resources for a New Century*, Philadelphia: University of Pennsylvania School of Social Work.

European Commission (1989a) 'Council Directive of 21 December 1988 on a general system for the recognition of higher-education diplomas on completion of professional education and training of at least 3 years', *Brussels Official Journal of the European Communities*, (24 January), European Commission (1989b) Proposal for a Council Directive on a second general system for the recognition of professional education and training with complements, Brussels: Directive 89/48 EEC of 21 December 1988,

Healy, L. M. (1986) 'The international dimension in social work education: current efforts, future challenges'. *International Social Work* 29(2): 135-147.

Horncastle, J. (1994) 'Training for international social work: initial experiences', *International Social Work* 37 (4): 309-318.

The existence of schemes such as ERASMUS and TEMPUS, which offer financial support for travel and subsistence, have facilitated the movement of staff and students between the member countries' higher educational institutions, and more widely. A debate has taken place concerning the advantages of a European dimension to social work training, and these do appear considerable, particularly for the small number of students who intend to take advantage of the opportunities to work in a foreign member state. The confirmation of the existence of a large number of commonalties, particularly in the value base of European practice, may strengthen a profession whose presentation and confidence have been weak. This

Europeanisation (and internationalisation) is increasing, and a major need is to establish a theoretical base from which to understand the process.

Horncastle, J. and Brobeck, H. (1995) 'An international perspective on practice teaching for foreign students' *Social Work in Europe* 2(3): 48-52.

Examines the results of small study, which looked at how practice teachers viewed the experience of supervising an exchange student from a different country. Questionnaires were circulated to a sample of Danish and English practice teachers and the results analysed. Concludes that despite the problems, practice teachers believe that they can offer a useful experience to foreign students, and the teachers themselves also feel they benefit from the placement.

Humphries, B. (1997) 'The dismantling of anti-discrimination in British social work: a view from social work education', *International Social Work* 40(3): 289-301.

Social work education in the UK underwent a government review during 1994/95. Central to this review is the dilution of the requirement on students to understand and confront institutionalised inequality in British society. This article discusses the significance of this by comparing the debates on 'political correctness in the USA and the UK. It identifies such debates as a contemporary moment in a longer history and examines contradictions in the rules and requirements governing social work education in the UK. It argues for a new radicalised agenda for social work education, which is not met by the review.

Huxtable, M. (1998) 'School social work: an international profession', *Social Work in Education* 20(2): 95-109.

This article provides a summary of the state of school social work around the world, including the scope and services of school social workers in 13 countries. The article examines how school social workers around the world are dealing with issues such as poor attendance, low achievement, and school violence. Similarities and differences in how the speciality has developed in various countries are described, common problems are noted, and areas of possible co-operation are suggested. The role of the school social work profession in the United States in international activities is examined.

Jack, G. and Jordan, B. (1998) 'Social work training in central and Eastern Europe: experiences in Bulgaria and Slovakia', *European Journal of Social Work* 1(2): 165-175.

The authors draw on their experiences as members of EU-funded projects for training social workers in post-communist countries to reflect on developments in social work education there, and in the United Kingdom. Argues that the emergence of social work in Central and Eastern Europe has a double agenda - to improve professional skills and values in the public services, and to contribute to the strengthening of a democratic and participatory civil society.

Jones, H. D. (1994) *Social Workers or Social Educators: The International Context for Developing Social Care*, London: National Institute for Social Work. International Centre (International Centre paper: no.2).

Comparative study of social work and social welfare in Europe, focusing on professional education, training institutions and the curriculum. Also includes a section on professional associations.

Kolleck, B. et al. (1993) 'Computers in social work education: a European perspective'. *New Technology in the Human Services* 7(1): 17-21.

Reviews the use of IT in social work education in the Netherlands, Germany and Denmark, and the need to incorporate social work values in the use of IT.

Korr, W. S., Fallon, B.J. and Brieland, D. (1994) 'UN convention to the rights of the child: implications for social work education', *International Social Work* 37(4): 333-345.

This paper first provides a conceptual model for children's rights as a framework for presenting the contents of the convention. For countries that are parties to the Convention, the model helps understand issues related to implementation. For countries still considering ratification, the model is a concise way to present the key provisions of the convention. It also facilitates introduction of the Convention into the social work curriculum as a primary source to make students aware of children's rights.

Lorenz, W. (1986) 'Social work education in Western Europe: themes and opportunities', *Issues in Social Work Education* 6(2): 89-100.

The paper surveys the present state of social work education in most of the countries of Western Europe in the context of the nascent internationalism which was destroyed by the advance of nazism in the 1930s. The themes considered are the status of social work within educational institutions, government recognition, practice content and evaluation, and the curriculum.

Lyons, K. (1989) 'The European dimension in social work training', *Issues in Social Work Education* 9(1and2): 93-99.

In this paper Lyons suggests that individuals and courses have much to gain from developing a wider perspective, and indeed have an increasing responsibility to take account of and incorporate at least a European dimension into social work education and training programmes. Lyons outlines some issues raised by 1992 and options open to social work educators in responding to them with a number of questions, including, is a British social work qualification equivalent to its European counterparts? How can we develop European perspectives in already overcrowded curricula?

Mohr, B. and Leibig, I. (1988) *Higher Education in the European Community* (fifth edition), Luxembourg: Publications of the European Communities.

Poster, C., and Kruger, A. (eds) (1990) *Community Education and The Western World,* London: Routledge.

Rachman, R. (1994) '"Teach me how to fish so that I can eat forever": an account of a joint Anglo-Armenian social work training project' *Social Work in Europe* 1(3): 17-24.

Describes a collaborative educational project involving staff and students from the Yerevan State University and the London School of Economics, the programme of teaching social work theory and practice, reflects upon issues from this transcultural experiences, and considers the implications for the development of social work in Armenia.

Rowlings, C. (1991) 'More than of academic interest: taking a European perspective on social work education', *Issues in Social Work Education* 11(1): 62-68.

All the member states in the European Community have a profession called social work for which training is available and usually required. Yet, there are differences in how the role is defined and in both the content and process of social work training. This paper describes some of these differences and raises questions about whether we should seek greater shortcomings of seeking Europe only in terms of the EC and in conclusion, expresses the hope that social work educators will play their part in the development of social work and social service in a rapidly changing Europe.

Schiller, H. (1983) 'Current situation and trends in European social work education', *International Social Work* 26(3): 1-6.

Shardlow, S. M. and Shardlow, P. (1993). *A Wider Vision for Post Qualifying Studies (In Europe: 4)*, London: Central Council for Education and Training in Social Work.

Identifies existing and potential links with European courses, looks at how UK and European PQ programmes can complement each other and explores how migrant social workers might participate in UK PQ programmes. Contains a country by country description of PQ studies in the EC and other European states, together with suggestions on how to develop links.

Tracy, M. B. (1992) 'Cross-national social-welfare policy analysis in the graduate curriculum - a comparative process model', *Journal of Social Work Education* 28(3): 341-352.

This article presents an analytical model for enabling social work graduate students to understand social welfare policies in a cross-national context. The author discusses a policy process model for comparative study that helps to explain why income, health, and social service programs are different among nations. The model examines governmental policies in other nations in terms of legal and assumed jurisdiction, obstacles and constraints to intervention, catalysts for intervention, needs identification, goals and strategies, program description, and evaluation.

Wagner, A. (1992) 'Social work education in an integrated Europe: pleas for a global perspective', *Journal of Teaching in Social Work* 6(2): 115-30.

In the consciousness of many Europeans, '1992' has assumed an almost mystical quality. The relatively slow pace of European integration - launched by the treaty of Rome in 1957 - was accelerated in the mid-eighties with the publication of the Single European Act (1986). The first part of this paper deals with the impact of these measures on 'social work', a concept which covers a widely diverse reality in Europe. The impact of European integration will be assessed with respect to social work education as well as social work practice. In the second part, a conceptual framework is developed, based on the idea of integration achieved through transactions of sharing, rather than transactions of exchange. In this context, the question is posed as to whether the international network of social work institutions (professional and educational), which today often functions as an instrument of exclusion, should not instead function as an instrument of inclusion. As a result of this discussion, a plan of action is developed, to transform the existing international network of social work from a rather 'exclusive' club to an all-inclusive international community.

Warchawiak, E. (1987) *Comparative Study of Training in Social Work in the European Community*, Brussels: Commission of the European Communities.

Watt, J. W. (1998) 'Social work education in the Baltic States and Poland: students assess their programs', *International Social Work* 41(1): 103-13.

Concern with use of educational methods which reflect the egalitarian underpinnings of social work is a major theme in the development of social work education programs in nations which have emerged from the domination of the former Soviet Union. Social work educators in the Baltic states with no tradition of professional social work, express particular interest in use of collegial styles of education. There is a clear recognition that learning occurs through the process of education as well as in content. Thus, any approach which contributes to creating greater exchange between social work faculty and social work students has great import for developing social work programs in Eastern Europe.

Watts, T. D., Elliott, D., Mayadas, N. S. and Bagley, C. (1997) 'International handbook on social work education [review]', *Journal of Comparative Family Studies* XXVIII: 167-168.

Williams, B. (1997) 'University-based social work education: quaint and dated?', *Canadian Social Work Review* 14(1): 69-82.

Discusses how there are moves afoot in the UK and across the industrialised world to replace academically based education for the professions with a narrower and more mechanistic form of training. Social workers in England and Wales, for example, have experienced an attempt to remove the initial education and training of probation officers from university social work programmes.

Williams, C. (1996) 'ERASMUS and SOCRATES in Koblenz: an alternative view', *Social Work in Europe* 3(3): 29-33.

Evaluates the ERASMUS and SOCRATES programmes of international co-operation in social work education.

Social work: general issues

Abrahamson, P. (1992) 'Poverty and welfare in Denmark', *Scandinavian Journal of Social Welfare* 1(1): 20-27.

From 1945 to the 1980s, Denmark was characterised by the absence of poverty or at least by the lack of any debate over poverty. However, by the mid-1980s, the presence of new forms of poverty made it impossible for politicians and social scientists to neglect poverty as an issue. The re- emergence of poverty did not clarify its extent, but it is widely agreed that poverty now is related to social exclusion and marginalization from the labour market. Empirical evidence is given that shows a poverty incidence of about 8%; the extent of marginalization is calculated to include 20-25% of the population of working age. The existence of poverty can be seen as a critique of the Scandinavian welfare state project, which was developed explicitly to fight and eliminate poverty. Concludes with a discussion of the latest welfare state development in Scandinavia and possible future trends, summarised as welfare pluralism.

Adams, A., Erath, P., and Shardlow, S. M. (eds.) (2000) *Fundamentals of Social Work in Selected European Countries: Present Theory, Practice, Perspectives, Historical and Practice Contexts* . Lyme Regis: Russell House.

How are global and European forces influencing society, social policy, social security systems and social work practice in the various countries of Europe? Are continued differences in policy and practice a response to specific current social problems, or an outcome of history and politics? In this groundbreaking book academics and practitioners write about social work in their own countries using a shared terminology, which is defined in a glossary, to facilitate comparison and learning from each other. Separate chapters cover historical and political contexts, present theories, practice and perspectives in: Finland, France, Czech Republic, Germany, Italy, Netherlands, Spain, UK. The editors' conclusion illustrates that although the debates in each country may sound familiar, there are both similarities and significant differences in context and outcome and therefore much that we can learn from each other.

Alber, J. (1995) 'A framework for the comparative study of social services', *Journal of European Social Policy* 5(2): 131-149.

> Comparative research on welfare states has most focused on social transfers as the dependent variable. As demographic changes make social services increasingly important ingredients of welfare state production, however, it will be necessary to shift the research agenda accordingly, and to take services more systematically into account. Building on Stein Rokkan's approach to the study of European political development, the article specifies some tasks for the comparative study of social services. Following a short overview of the topics and phases of comparative welfare state research, it proposes a set of variables for the mapping of variations in service supply as well as a check list of variables which might help to explain such variations. The new research perspective is then applied to a comparative analysis of services for elderly people in European countries, which is based on a re-analysis of the country reports for the European Commission's Observatory on Older People in Europe.

Alexander, C.A. (1985) 'Contradictions of contemporary society and social work ethics', *International Social Work* 28(3): 1-7

Anttonen A. and Sipila, J. (1996) 'European social care services: is it possible to identify models?', *Journal of European Social Policy* 6(2): 87-100.

> The purpose of this article is to bring social care services into the domain of comparative social policy research. The reason why it is important for social care services to be incorporated into the debate is that they represent an expanding component of the welfare state; that they are important for women; that there are major differences between different countries in social care services. The authors have defined social care services as a specific way of increasing autonomy of both care providers and care receivers. Two distinct models of social care services emerge from the analysis of service volumes and state policies; two, possibly, three other models remain more tentative. These models seem to offer very different options and opportunities as regards women's gainful employment and care solutions outside the family.

Backman, G. and Sharma, S. (1998) 'Changing social welfare systems in the Nordic nations: some observations and analyses', New *Global Development: Journal of International and Comparative Social*

Welfare, 14 (1): 33-45.

This article attempts to provide some observations and analyses of the changing social welfare systems in the Nordic nations.

Beck, W., van der Maesen, L. and Walker, A. (1998) *The Social Quality of Europe,* Bristol: The Policy Press.

This book focuses on the essential questions concerning the future of the European Union. It introduces an entirely new concept to European discourse - social quality - which is intended to create a fresh point of departure for debate. Included are critical commentaries and syntheses focusing on employment, social protection, social exclusion and provision for older people.

Bennike, M. (1998) 'Post traumatic stress disorder: social work at a Danish rehabilitation centre for refugees', *Social Work in Europe* 5(1): 24-28.

Describes the work of a rehabilitation centre for refugees in Denmark.

Bergman, M. (1991) 'The emerging voluntary sector in Eastern Europe' *Euronews*, (7) (December): 3.

Brief notes on the growing voluntary sector response to the needs of older people in Eastern Europe, and the work of the author's organisation HelpAge International.

Bradley, G. and Harris, R. (1993) 'Social work in Europe: an ERASMUS initiative', *Social Work Education* 12(3): 51-66.

A number of social work institutions have mounted and sustained consistent exchange programmes with European institutions and this is a report of an aspect of these exchanges, a Four-Nation Seminar.

Bradley, G., Kahl, W., and Clarke, C. (1995) 'Anti-oppressive practice and social work in Europe', *Social Work Education* 14(2): 5-10.

This paper offers a résumé of discussions held with students and colleagues at a Colloque Quadri-National in Marseilles. Whilst the views recorded are impressionistic and cannot do justice to the complex debates and cultural context from which they are plucked, nonetheless they help to provide a snapshot (albeit subjective) of what is happening in some key cities in Europe with regard to the practice and training of anti-oppressive ideas.

Bradshaw, J. and Chen J-R. (1997) 'Poverty in the UK. A comparison with nineteen other countries', *Benefits - a Journal of Social Security, Research, Policy and Practice* 18(January): 13-17.

> This article compares poverty in 20 countries. The countries covered include Australia, Belgium, Canada, Czech Republic, Denmark, Finland, Germany, Hungary, Israel, Italy, Netherlands, Norway, Poland, Russia, Slovakia, Spain, Sweden, Taiwan UK and USA. The text looks in particular at poverty risks, the composition of the poor, sensitivity of the poverty threshold, inequality and general trends.

Bradshaw, J., and Terum, L.I. (1997) 'How Nordic is the Nordic model? Social assistance in a comparative perspective' *Scandinavian Journal of Social Welfare*, 6(4): 247-256.

> Explores how Nordic countries are often perceived as representing a special type of welfare state. This article focuses on arrangements directed towards poor and marginalised people, which in most country are social assistance schemes. Argues that it is difficult to distinguish particular Nordic approach for two reasons. Concludes by identifying an approach towards poor and marginalised people that is common in small, communitarian affluent and homogenous countries.

Brawley, E. A. and Schindler R. (1989) 'Professional-paraprofessional relationships in four countries: a comparative analysis', *International Social Work* 32(2): 91-106.

> A study of four countries - Britain, India, Israel and the USA - was carried out to assess the tensions that exist in professional-paraprofessional relations and to identify conditions that tend to foster constructive relationships.

Campfens, H. (ed.) (1997) *Community Development Around the World: Practice, Theory, Research, Training*, Toronto: University of Toronto Press.

> This is a comparative study looking at the theory and practice of community development and goes on to focus on: Canada; the Netherlands; Israel; Ghana; Bangladesh; and Chile.

Cannan, C., Berry, L. and Lyons, K. (1992) *Social Work and Europe*, Basingstoke: Macmillan.

> Aims to place British social work in the framework of 'social Europe' and to identify some of the emerging European social work issues, policies and trends. Deals primarily with attitudes

and ways of thinking about the social work task rather then legislative and political details, and draws on practice in areas of France and Germany to make suggestions for the direction of social work in the 1990s.

CCETSW (1989) *Report from the European Directive Workshop* Stoke Rochford, London: Central Council for Education and Training in Social Work.

Cemlyn, S. (1995) 'Social work in Russia and the UK: what are we exchanging?', *Social Work Education* 14(1): 77-92.

Links between British and Russian social work agencies and training courses are increasing, opening up both mutual opportunities and challenges. Describes the experience of the author and others during recent visits as guests of a social work course in St Petersburg. It explores what was learnt about the underpinnings, aspirations and struggles of the emerging social work profession in Russia, and the effect on us as British social work professionals. It explores cross-cultural and ethical issues, and considers questions which arise for the future of exchange schemes. These include the complex relationship between the export of political ideology and economic systems to former Soviet countries, and the export of welfare ideology and methods.

Cemlyn, S. and Vdovenko, T. (1995) 'Working with street children in St. Petersburg', *Social Work in Europe* 2(2): 15-23.

This article is based on a tripartite East-West partnership developing social work education in St. Petersburg. It outlines the scale, manifestations and causes of the phenomenon of street children in St. Petersburg, and reviews aspects of the existing local state system for working with children in difficulties. Its primary focus is the developing work of non-governmental organisations; similar and divergent themes in their aims, methods and organisational development are examined through five case examples, which are compared with the findings of a Council of Europe study. It concludes with a consideration of the national context, international links, and future policy and practice developments.

Chamberlayne, P. (1992) 'New directions in welfare? France, West Germany, Italy and Britain in the 1980's', *Critical Social Policy* 33 (Winter): 5-21.

Introduces debates about the future of welfare, particularly systems of income maintenance, and identifies two axes of debate: the first economic, concerned with responses to labour market restructuring, challenges to the insurance-assistance divide, and demands that 'care' be rewarded as 'work' and secondly, concerning social relations of welfare - bureaucratisation, empowerment and strengthening the 'social'.

Clasen, J. (ed.) (1997) *Social Insurance in Europe,* Bristol: The Policy Press.

This study of social insurance schemes across Europe asks several questions. What are the institutional and political forces that have shaped national systems? Are national governments diminishing the role of social insurance Does social insurance have a future or is it an outdated welfare arrangement?, Can the UK learn from experiences elsewhere?. By illustrating similarities and differences within and across countries, this book reflects on the current role of social insurance, recent policy changes and pressures for reform in 10 European countries: UK, France, Germany, Switzerland, Greece, Portugal, Czech Republic, Hungary, Sweden and Denmark.

Clasen, J., Gould, A. and Vincent, J. (1998) *Voices Within and Without,* Bristol: The Policy Press.

This text examines in depth the situation of the long term unemployed, painting a picture of low long term unemployment is tackled, how it is perceived and how it is experienced within a comparative perspective. The study contrasts the welfare state regimes in Germany, Sweden and Great Britain, giving insight into different types of policies and their perceived effectiveness regarding both labour market integration and issues of social inclusion, individual autonomy and self esteem.

Cochrane, A. and Clarke, J. (1993) *Comparing Welfare States,* Milton Keynes: Open University Press.

Commission of the European Communities (1991) *ECTS Review of First Year of Operation 1989/90*, Brussels: ERASMUS Bureau.

Council of Europe Study Group of the 1978 Co-ordinated Research Fellowships Programme (1980) *New Forms in the Structures and Organisation of Social Services, Including Multidisciplinary Centres and Systems to encourage Client Participation,* Strasbourg: Council of Europe.

Council of Europe (1987) *Proceedings of the Joint Meeting on Human Rights and Social Workers,* Strasbourg: Council of Europe.

Cousins, C. (1998) 'Social exclusion in Europe: paradigms of social disadvantage in Germany, Spain, Sweden and the United Kingdom', *Policy and Politics* 26(2): 127-146.

> This article reviews contemporary discussions of the concept of social exclusion in Europe and examines different paradigms of inclusion and exclusion in selected Europe countries. A central concern of the article is to link the literature on social exclusion with the debate on welfare regimes and labour market structures, and mechanisms of social protection. Drawing on recent comparative analyses the article also considers how women and ethnic minority groups, as well as different social classes, are included or excluded in different welfare regimes.

Cox, C. (1992) 'Expanding social work's role in home care: an ecological perspective', *Social Work* 37(2): 179-183.

> Summarises characteristics of home care services in the U.S.A., England, Sweden and Norway.

Daly, M. (1997) 'Welfare states under pressure: cash benefits in European welfare states over the last ten years', *Journal of European Social Policy* 7(2): 129-146.

> This article looks at the substance of welfare reform in Europe over the course of the last 10 years. It compares how cash transfers in the member states of the European Union as well as Norway have fared over the decade. Observes that pensions, unemployment benefits, parental leave and payments for the care of the ill, elderly and incapacitated have been the main focus of policy activity. Considers how to make analytical frameworks equal to the richness of the reform process which is under way.

Deacon, B. and Szalai, J. (eds) (1990) *Social Policy in the New Europe*, Aldershot: Avebury.

Deacon, B. et al. (eds) (1992) *The New Eastern Europe*, London: Sage.

Deacon, B. (1992) 'Social welfare developments in Eastern Europe and the future for socialist welfare' in Carter, P. et al. *Changing Social Work and Welfare*. Buckingham: Open University Press.

Dearling, A. (1997) 'New travellers in Europe', *Social Work in Europe* 4(3): 34-39.

This article offers a number of insights into the lives and aspirations of one of the UK's most demonised and marginalised groups: new Travellers.

Deleeck, H., Van den Bosch K. (1992) 'Poverty and adequacy of social security in Europe: a comparative analysis', *Journal of European Social Policy* 2(2): 107-120.

Reports the findings of a collective research project in seven countries and regions in the EC, which aimed to establish in a comparative way, the number of poor households in each country, to identify social groups at high risk of poverty, and to assess the adequacy of social security in guaranteeing a minimum income.

Dixon, J. and Scheurell, R. P. (eds) (1989) *Social welfare in Developed Market Countries*, London: Routledge.

Analyses social welfare systems in the following countries: Australia, Canada, West Germany, Italy, the Netherlands, New Zealand, Norway, Sweden, the United Kingdom and the United States of America. It considers, for each of these countries and in a standard format, the underlying ideological / value framework of the social welfare systems, describes the historical evolution of the systems and examines the political, social and economic context of the systems. Each chapter looks at the structure and administration of the systems, and how they are financed. This is followed by a consideration of the nature of the different parts of the welfare system, a survey of social security, personal social services and the treatment of key groups: the aged, the disabled and handicapped, the young, needy families, the unemployed and the sick and injured. Each chapter concludes with an assessment of the effectiveness of the system considered.

Elliot, D, Mayadas, N. S. and Watts, T.D. (1990) *The World of Social Welfare: Social Welfare and Services in an International Context,* Springfield, Il: Charles C. Thomas.

Esping-Andersen, G. (1997) 'Hybrid or unique?: the Japanese welfare state between Europe and America', *Journal of European Social Policy* 7(3): 179-189.

Looks at how in the contemporary welfare state literature, Japan and Southern Europe are often held to be distinct regimes.

Provides a comparative examination of the evidence for Japan and argues that any attempt at labelling the Japanese welfare state is premature since it has not yet sunk its roots.

Estes, J. E. (1996) 'Social work, social development and community welfare centres in international perspective', *International Social Work* 40 (1): 43-55.

The 'community' and 'community development' practice always have been at the conceptual centre of social work practice in urban areas. The reasons for this are threefold: (1) community work seeks to unite previously unorganised people into effective groups and coalitions that work together in pursuit of a shared social agenda; (2) community work seeks to strengthen traditional family, kinship and neighbourhood ties in the community and to develop new social arrangements that are essential to the effective functioning of communities; and (3) community based social services are among the most effective and cost efficient approaches serving the poor. In addition to these functions it has been suggested that community development is an essential ingredient in the success of democratic societies.

European Seminar of Heads of Welfare Agencies (1984) *Papers on Community care*, Uxbridge: Association of Directors of Social Services.

Papers from a DHSS/EEC funded seminar. Contents: welcome address (H. Laming), social policy in the EEC (D. Grennan), community care in Sweden (H. Swedner), work of the EEC with disabled people (P.Daunt), policy options in the PSS (R.Pinker), care of children and the family in Belgium (L.M. Bataille), community care of the elderly in the Federal Republic of Germany (I. Gaertner), social effects of large-scale unemployment (B. Roycroft).

European Forum (1994): *Social Exclusion in Different Fields of Social Work*; Bonn: Paritatische.

Summary of the findings of a conference held on 13/14 November 1993 in Brussels on social exclusion. Includes papers on: EC actions on social exclusion; social exclusion in France, the United Kingdom and Germany; exchanges of experience through partnerships; and working parties to develop strategies.

Falck, H.S. (1996) 'Social welfare and social work: self-help and social exchange', *Scandinavian Journal of Social Welfare* 5(3): 54-158.

This article explores the ambiguities and ambivalences of the subject of social welfare in the majority of European-based societies including the United States. The central argument of this article is that societies are organised consistent with either an exchange model of social welfare or a societal self-help model.

Flora, P. and Heidenheimer, A. (eds) (1981) *The Development of Welfare States in Europe and America*, New Brunswick: Transaction.

Forte, J. A. (1994) 'Around the world with social group work: knowledge and research contributions', *Social Work with Groups* 17(1-2): 143-62.

This article uses a quantitative content analysis to assess the contribution of international group workers toward building a scientific knowledge base for practice. Using AASWG's bibliography as a sampling frame, 271 articles written between 1978 and 1992 by group workers employed outside the United States were studied. It was found that 38% were scientific knowledge building articles. Narrative descriptions of group work dominated the literature. Four countries, Australia, Canada, Great Britain and Israel were sites for the bulk of the publications. Each showed emphases in their group work writings reflective of cultural and social particulars.

Friedlander, W. A. (1975) *International Social Welfare*, Englewood Cliffs, NJ: Prentice-Hall.

Friedmann, R. R., Gilbert, N. and Sherer, M. (eds) (1987) *Modern Welfare States: A Comparative View of Trends and Prospects*, London: Wheatsheaf, pp. 44-82.

Giarchi, G.G. and Lankshear, G. (1998) 'The eclipse of social work in Europe', *Social Work in Europe* 5(3): 25.

This paper attempts to discover the extent to which social work has been eclipsed in Europe. It deals with the problem of defining social work and focus upon care functions of social workers within 'greater Europe'. It will ascertain to what extent social work in Europe has maintained its status and/or been made redundant, and to what extent it has been replaced by non-social workers in the voluntary or private sectors.

Ginn, J. and Arber, S. (1992) 'Towards women's independence: pension systems in three contrasting European welfare states', *Journal of European Social Policy* 2(4): 255-277.

The treatment of women as family dependents by state social security systems in industrialised societies has become increasingly problematic due to trends over the last 50 years such as the rise in cohabitation, divorce and lone parenthood and women's increased participation in the paid labour force. These developments, together with anxieties about the public cost of pensions in countries with an ageing population, have promoted re- examination of pension systems, and moves towards treating women as individuals responsible for providing their own financial support in later life. Whilst this is an advance in terms of women's formal equality with men, there is a danger that women will suffer by these changes if social policies are not enacted to enable them to obtain adequate pensions in their own right. Examines the pension systems of the UK, Germany and Denmark to assess the extent to which each treats women as financially independent individuals, and how each pension system in combination with the predominant pattern of women's employment, affects women's pension acquisition.

Gould, A. (1993) 'Opposition to syringe exchange schemes in the UK and Sweden', *Journal of European Social Policy* 3(2): 107-118.

In 1988 official reports in England and Wales and Sweden recommended the widespread adoption of syringe exchange schemes to reduce the risk of HIV infection amongst intravenous drug users. The British government accepted the recommendation and by the end of 1989, 120 such schemes had been established in England alone. The Swedish government did not accept the recommendation and by the end of 1980 the only schemes operating with official recognition were those in the cities of Lund and Malmo, on which the official report in Sweden had originally been based. This paper argues that the factors explaining these contrasting outcomes involve a number of inter-relating professional, institutional, historical and cultural differences between the two countries which have made the care and treatment of misusers in the UK a de-politicised and technical matter for professionals, while in Sweden it is a highly politicised one, bound up with issues of national identity and character.

Gough, I. (1997) 'Social assistance in OECD countries', *Journal of European Social Policy* 7(1): 17-43.

This article presents selected results from the first comparative study of social assistance across all countries of the OECD. The scope of social assistance, discussed in the first section, is drawn to include all means- tested benefits in cash and kind, including those which provide benefits to higher income groups. The second section then presents information on the main programmes in each country, expenditures and groups of beneficiaries, trends over time, administrative structures, and operation of means tests. The third section, distils from the country differences eight patterns, or 'assistance regimes', varying from the limited, discretionary, decentralised models of Switzerland and Norway to the extensive, national, rights-based programmes of the English speaking world; and from the relative generosity of Scandinavia and Australia to the low, marginalising benefits of the Mediterranean countries and the USA. The last section turns to the economic pressures and political debates which are driving contemporary policy changes.

Gould, A. (1993) *Capitalist Welfare Systems: A Comparison of Japan, Britain and Sweden*, London: Longman.

Grebel, H. and Steyaert, J. (1995) 'Social informatics: beyond technology. A research project in schools of social work in the European community', *International Social Work* 38 (2): 151-64.

The introduction of information technology (IT) in human services has been a slow and tedious process and its impact on service provision has been slow. As a consequence, the introduction of IT as a subject in the curricula of social work schools has been slow as well. For a number of reasons, there have been dramatic changes in this situation over the past few years. This article provides an overview of the main areas in which IT is being applied in service provision across Europe.

Hadley, R. and Leidy, B. (1996) 'Community social work in a market environment: a British-American exchange of technologies and experience', *British Journal of Social Work* 26(6): 823-842.

Community social work, which flourished in Britain in the late 1970s and through much of the 1980s, has been sidelined in recent years by the combined development of market-oriented policies and managerialism. However, certain recent initiatives in human services in the USA, a country which has moved far further towards a contract culture than Britain, show that some American practitioners are increasingly critical of the perceived limitations of their own system and are now seeking to borrow from earlier British experience in making it more integrated, localised and community-oriented. This article explores the example of an American county human services agency which has moved in this direction and considers its relevance for the survival and future development of community oriented social work and social services in the quasi-market environment which is emerging in Britain.

Harris, R. and Lavan, A. (1992) 'Professional mobility in the new Europe: the case of social work', *Journal of European Social Policy* 2(1): 1-15.

Freedom of movement for professionals within the European Community is to be attained by means of an EC directive which visits upon member states the obligation to recognise Higher Education Diplomas awarded by other member states as equivalent to their own. The introduction and implementation of the relevant directive (89/48/EEC) are described, and a number of issues identified which seem likely to affect its success. In particular certain complexities, both conceptual and operational, are discussed, and it is argued that formidable obstacles must be overcome if the system is to be introduced effectively and economically. A brief history and account of the directive system follows, demonstrating why the particular approach used in directive 89/48/EEC came into being. The implementation procedures are outlined and some further questions are posed.

Harris, R. (1990) 'Beyond rhetoric: a challenge for international social work', *International Social Work* 33(3): 204-12.

Hayward, B. (1990) *A Perspective for a Global Approach: The Social Action Programmes of the EC*, Paris: Interim Report to EC.

Hayward, R. (1996) 'The work of the Hamlet Trust in Central and Eastern Europe' *Social Work in Europe* 3(3): 12-18.

Heady, C. (1997) 'Labour market transitions and social exclusion', *Journal of European Social Policy* 7(2): 119-128.

This article considers the dynamic effects that the labour market has on poverty and social exclusion. It shows how the analysis of labour markets can help our understanding of social exclusion and reviews some of the evidence from Europe and the United States.

Henderson, P. and Scott, T. (1988) *The circonscription system in French social services: its relevance to the UK*, London: Economic and Social Research Council.

Research which studied a particular aspect of French social service organisation - 'circonscription', in particular the role of the 'responsable', who plays a co-ordinating role between agencies.

Henderson, P. and Scott, T. (1990) 'Making the most of 1992'. *Community Care* (801): 20-21.

Reports on research into aspects of social services provision in France, which highlighted aspects of their work from which British SSDs might learn.

Hill, M. (ed.) (1991) *Social Work and the European Community: The Social Policy and Practice Contexts*, London: Jessica Kingsley.

Analyses the similarities and differences in approaches to public welfare, social service organisation, and social work education within the social and political contexts of the European Community. Includes more specific chapters on: responses to child abuse in the EC; services to elderly people in Belgium, France, West Germany and the Republic of Ireland; and services to families with young children in Denmark.

Hokenstad, M. C., Khinduka, S. K. and Midgley, J. (eds) (1992) *Profiles in International Social Work*, Washington DC: National Association of Social Workers.

Hokenstad, M C, Khinduka, S. K., Midgley, J. and Swedner, H. (eds) (1993) 'Profiles in international social work, *Scandinavian Journal of Social Welfare* 2(3): 172-173.

Hume, S. (1998) 'Paradox in professional practice - women's' views of social work: a tri-national study in England, Germany and Italy', *European Journal of Social Work* 1(1): 55-70.

This article describes an international comparative study which highlights some of the dilemmas and tensions inherent in social work practice presented by women working in three European countries: Italy, Germany and England. Examines the extent to which factors such as women's roles, caring and gender difference impacted upon work styles, practice and management in social work and on policy development in the personal social services.

Jack, R. (1996) 'Knee jerk journalism about social work in Romania and Britain', *Social Work in Europe* 3(1): 40-42.

Gives an optimistic account of the present state of social work and social welfare in Romania. Looks in particular at recent initiatives in social work education which are helping to re-assert social work as a profession in Romania which has the respect of its population. Also argues that social work in the UK could benefit from a more supportive environment.

Jones, C. (ed.) (1993) *New perspectives on the Welfare State in Europe*, London: Routledge.

Part I. One the state of the art. 1. Rudolf Klein. O'Goffe's tale - or what can we learn from the success of the capitalist welfare states? 2. Ramesh Mishra. Social policy in the postmodern world. Part II. Issues from Britain. 3. Jonathan Bradshaw. Developments in social security policy. 4. John Doling. Encouraging home ownership. 5. Nicholas Deakin. Privatism and partnership in urban policy. 6. Jaqi Nixon and Valerie Williamson. Returned and retainer polcies for women. Part III. Prospects for Europe. 7. Stephan Leibfried. Towards a European welfare state? On integrating poverty regimes into the European Community. 8. Arthur Gould. The end of the middle way? The Swedish welfare state in crisis. 9. Bob Deacon. Developments in East European social policy. 10. Catherine Jones. The Pacific challenge - Confucian welfare states. Part IV. On the state of the argument. 11. Richard Rose. Bringing freedom back in.

Jones, C. (1985) *Patterns of Social Policy: An Introduction to Comparative Analysis*, London: Tavistock.

Kangas, O. (1994) 'The merging of welfare state models? Past and present trends in Finnish and Swedish social policy', *Journal of European Social Policy* 4(2): 72-94.

Recent social policy debates have revolved around different typologies of the welfare states. Although these typologies portray large historical trends, empirical tests of the existence of the welfare state models are often based on cross-sectional inspections. For several reasons, cross- sectional analyses may give biased results. This paper assesses longitudinal patterns in social policy formulation in Finland, Germany, Sweden, and the United Kingdom, each representing a different variant of social policy models. In particular, the paper deals with historical trends and present problems of the Scandinavian model of social policy. The historical review studies whether the Nordic countries ever shared a common pattern of social policy.

The examination of present-day challenges discusses whether

current policy responses make these countries more similar to other countries.

Kazi, M.A., Mantysaari, M. and Rostila I. (1997) 'Promoting the use of single-case designs: social work experiences from England and Finland', *Research on Social Work Practice* 7(3): 311-328.

Critically analyses the use of single-case evaluation by social work practitioners in Finland and England. Examines the experiences from both countries where attempts were made by academic researchers to encourage social workers to use single-case designs in the evaluation of their practice. The interventions used by the researchers in the universities at Tampere in Finland and Huddersfield in England to promote the use of single-case evaluation by practitioners are described in detail to enable replication and to develop the potential to learn from the interventions used by others.

Knapp, M., Monserrat, J. and Fenyo, A. (1990) *Inter-sectoral and international contracting-out of long term care: evidence on comparative costs and efficiency from Britain and Spain,* Canterbury: University of Kent. Personal Social Services Research Unit.

Investigates relative cost efficiency in England and Wales and Catalunya, the reasons for cross-country differences and the longer-term role of the voluntary sectors.

Kornbeck, J. (1997) 'Community care in the United Kingdom, subsidiarity in Germany: only a matter of words?', *Social Work in Europe* 4(2): 1-11.

The article examines recent critiques of Community Care in the UK and compares the findings with similar critiques against Germany's concept of subsidiarity. Both were created to strengthen and empower society's micro-level, but were instrumentalised to serve the needs of the macro-level. Argues that it is not local authorities and clients, but rather central authorities that have benefited from these changes. Looks at how while the doctrines are dissimilar, their practical impact does seem alike.

Kornbeck, J. (1998) 'Researching social work professionalisation in the context of European integration', *Social Work in Europe* 5(3): 37.

This research report reviews a number of comparative works on social policy and social work in the EU and some other European states, and asks the place of professionalisation have in these materials.

Kramer, R. M. et al. (1993) *Privatisation in Four European Countries: Comparative Studies in Government-Third Sector Relationships*, New York: M.E. Sharpe.

Focuses on how four countries use voluntary non-profit organisations to provide services to people with disabilities and looks at the changing role of the voluntary or 'third' sector in welfare states. Also provides a comparative study of privatisation in the context of using non-governmental organisations to implement public policy.

Krivine, N. (1994) 'Responding to racism: a comparison of the French and English probation service' *Social Work in Europe* 1(2): 62-64.

Brief notes on a research project to compare anti-racism in the Probation Service in France and the UK, with personal reaction to the major cultural differences with regard to race between the two countries.

Lasok, D. (1986) *The Professions and Services in the European Economic Community*, Netherlands: Kluwer.

Leaper, R. A. B. (1988) 'Cash and care in a European perspective' in Becker, S., and MacPherson, S. (eds) *Public Issues Private Pain,* London: Insight.

Lesnik, B. (ed.) (1997) *International Perspectives in Social Work: Change in Social Work*, Aldershot, Hampshire: Ashgate.

Lesnik, B. (ed.) (1998) *International Perspectives in Social Work: Countering Discrimination in Social Work*, Aldershot, Hampshire: Ashgate.

Lesnik, B. (ed.) (1999) *International Perspectives in Social Work: Social Work and the State*, Brighton: Pavillion.

Lorenz, W. (1998) 'The ECSPRESS Approach - The social professions between national and global perspectives', *Social Work in Europe* 5(3):1-8

The Thematic Network for the Social Professions ECSPRESS (European Consortium of Social Professions with educational and Social Studies) had been set up to examine the possibilities of a shared European perspective in the social professions. However, all partners in this consortium, which comprises the major European organisations in the training and practice of social work and social pedagogy, had always been critical of any harmonisation of courses and the imposition of European standards.

Lorenz, W. (1994) *Social Work in a Changing Europe*, London: Routledge.

Lyons, K. (1999) *International Social Work: Themes and Perspectives*, Aldershot, Hampshire: Ashgate.

Mitchell, D. (1994) 'East greets West', *Community Care* 1040:24.

Russia has never had a system of social services, but over the past few years a network of collaboration has been built up between social workers in Russia and the UK. Early exchanges between Norfolk SSD and the Russians has culminated in the formation of the Russian European Trust for Welfare Reform.

Monkhouse, A. and Hetherington, R. (1997) 'Assessment and allocation in England and France: who decides?', *Social Work in Europe* 4(1): 46-49.

Compares the way in which local authority social services departments in England and France manage their day-to-day decision making.

Munday, B. (ed.) (1989) *The Crisis in Welfare States: An International Perspective on Social Services and Social Work*, Hemel Hampstead: Harvester Wheatsheaf.

Munday, B. (ed.) (1990) *Social Services in the EC and the Implications of 1992*, Canterbury: University of Kent.

Munday, B. (ed.) (1992) *Social Services in the Member States of the European Community: a Handbook of Information and Data,* Canterbury: European Institute of Social Services, University of Kent.

Thirteen chapters (twelve member states, but with individual chapters on the Flemish and French communities of Belgium) follow a common structure, introducing and putting into context social services systems, the organisation, responsibility and financing of social services, an inventory of services for each client group, and addresses of major governmental, statutory and voluntary and private agencies.

Munday, B. (1993) *European Social Services*, Canterbury: European Institute of Social Services, University of Kent.

Munday, B. (1996) *Social Care in Europe*, London: Prentice Hall.

Nordlund, A. (1997) 'Attitudes towards the welfare state in the Scandinavian countries', *Scandinavian Journal of Social Welfare* 6(4): 233-246.

Analyses whether Scandinavian's support for the welfare state has played a critical role in the transition of social policy. Based on surveys from Sweden, Norway and Denmark, two conclusions are reached. Also attempts to further the research on the relationship between institutional characteristics and attitudes. Concludes that institutional characteristics provide a reliable guidance for an understanding of attitudes toward social policy in the Scandinavian countries.

O'Cinneide, S. et al. (1994) *Social exclusion in Europe*. Helsinki: National Research and Development Centre for Welfare and Health.

Otis, J. (1986) 'The transferability of western social work across national boundaries: fact or fiction?' *Journal of International and Comparative Social Work* 2(1): 37-45.

The basic question is whether Western social work education should be transferred across national and cultural boundaries. The argument against such transfer has two major foundations: empirical and philosophical. The empirical argument holds that Western realities differ markedly from those in Third World countries. Therefore, Western social work knowledge and techniques are not applicable. The philosophical argument is based upon the assumptions of cultural relativism, which maintains that each culture is a unique reality whose values are worthwhile in themselves. Therefore, the transfer of Western social work education and practice, by definition, is a form of imperialism, an unwarranted imposition upon Third World values. That Western knowledge and values may be faulty is true, but that is a case to be made and not merely assumed. Cultural relativism is critiqued as a significant ideological impediment to dealing with the complex, practical problems of transferability. The general applicability of Western social work education and values is reviewed and the critical problem identified as a failure to make such knowledge and practice country specific.

Oyen, E. (ed.) (1986) *Comparing Welfare States and their Futures*, Aldershot: Gower.

Looks at the crises facing welfare states in a number of countries from a social science perspective, arguing that social welfare systems can not be studies without appreciating the importance of the major social change occurring in all countries. Argues that there are the same underlying processes which guide the future of welfare states, regardless of their cultural context or their stage of development. Common trends and problems are identified, including changes in class structure, institutional crises, the role of women, and demographic changes. Trends and problems in specific systems are discussed: formal and informal aspects of social welfare in Japan and Britain; welfare state regression in Scandinavia; changing Hungarian social policy; the New Zealand welfare state; the Austrian welfare state; debureaucratisation and the self-help movement in the Federal Republic of West Germany; the Kenyan welfare state; the Sri Lankan welfare state.

Payne, M. (1995) 'Social work and Europe', *British Journal of Social Work* 25(4): 537-544.

Payne, M., and Shardlow, S. M. (eds) (1998) *Contemporary Issues in Social Work: Western Europe*, Aldershot: Arena.

Patterson, D. A. (1996) 'An electronic social work knowledge base: a strategy for global information sharing', *International Social Work* 39 (2): 149-61.

Paper-based transmission of information is no longer adequate to meet the demands of the rapidly changing international environments in which social work is practised. If the social work profession is to be a viable participant in addressing global social challenges in the twilight of this millennium, it is essential that a strategy for electrical information sharing be set forth. The establishment of an international electronic social work knowledge base linking social work educators and professionals would allow for the rapid dissemination of vital information and the formation of global partnerships. The purpose of this paper is to present a rationale and conceptual design for the creation of this social work international information linkage (SWIRL) and describe its functions.

Pleiger, D. (1989/90) 'Case studies on social work in health care: a summary, *Eurosocial* (55/56): 27-33.An issues paper based on case studies conducted in Denmark, Hungary, Italy and Scotland.

Potucek, M. (1993) 'Current social policy developments in the Czech and Slovak Republics', *Journal of European Social Policy* 3(3): 209-226.

Both in the Czech Republic and Slovakia, social policy is at a crossroads. Having inherited many techniques and features of the Communist past, it must contend with rapidly changing economic and political conditions while its experts seek new orientations, priorities and instruments. Considered here are recent developments in industrial relations and employment policy, social security, medical care, housing, education, social support and care.

Rasmussen, H.C. and Pijl, M.A. (1994) *Some reflections on Social Development in Europe - a contribution to the UN Social Summit,* New York: ICSW European Region Bulletin (Special Issue).

Chapters: Integrating the excluded - policies and poverty and exclusion in Denmark; Achievements of social policy and future threats to social integration in Finland; Lutter contre la pauvret, et promouvoir l'integration sociale en France; The fight against poverty, unemployment and lack of integration in Germany; Social transformation in Eastern Europe; the Norwegian welfare state, a 40-year old experiment - What ought to be changed during the 90s?; The concept of poverty and forms of poverty; The Swedish model - dead, still alive or in transition?; Enhancing social integration through social care (UK); Social policies, from the individual to the world level by way of conclusions; Some reflections about social development in Western Europe.

Ritter, G. A. (1986) *Social Welfare in Britain and Germany*, Leamington Spa: Berg.

Rogge, M.E. and Darkwa, O. K. (1996) 'Poverty and the environment: an international perspective for social work', International *Social Work* 39 (4): 395-409.

The relationship between poverty and the environment is so vast that no single article can capture all its dimensions. In this paper, attention is focused on one kind and source of poverty, the plight of exploited people in exploited nations. Environmental problems facing the poor are reviewed by examining how the international trade in toxic waste has aggravated their living conditions. As a framework to illustrate these dynamics, Durning's three-tier model of the 'global poverty trap' is used. Last, strategies are suggested for social workers to intervene in the relationship between poverty and the environment.

Ronge, V. (1991) 'Social change in Eastern Europe: implications for the Western poverty agenda', *Journal of European Social Policy* 1(1): 49-56.

Room, G. (ed.) (1991) *Towards a European Welfare State*, Bristol: School for Advanced Urban Studies.

Room, G. et al. (1993) *Anti-Poverty Action-Research in Europe*, Bristol: School for Advanced Urban Studies.

Derives from the work of the evaluation team which worked within the second European Community Programme to Combat Poverty (1986-1989). The team, co-ordinated by the Centre for the Analysis of Social Policy at the University of Bath, working under contract to the ISG Sozialforschung und Gesellschaftspolitik, a social research institute itself under contract to the Commission of the European Communities to develop an Animation and Dissemination Service for the Programme. Reports on the evaluation of projects in a variety of member states under the themes: integrated action in urban areas; integrated action in rural areas; long-term unemployment; young unemployed; older people; single parent families; migrants; marginals.

Samualsson, G. and Brink, S. (1996) 'Quality attributes of home help services in Sweden and Canada - a consumer view', *Scandinavian Journal of Social Welfare*, 6(2): 82-90.

Describes of a survey of users evaluation of home help services in Sweden and Canada. The policy implications of the results for the future are discussed.

Seibel, F. W. and Lorenz, W. (eds) (1997) *The European Integration of Social Professions* . Koblenz: ECCE, CD ROM.

Sipila, J. (1995) 'Financial support for informal care in Britain, Finland and Michigan: a comparison of system functions', *International Social Work* 38(2): 177-189.

Carer's allowances are paid to non-professional carers for looking after a person at home. Support systems for informal care date back to the 1940s, but recent changes in the supply and demand of informal care have resulted in the creation of new administrative organizations in many countries. Carer's allowances are a peculiar form of social benefit in that they are based both on carrying out a specific assignment and on other criteria. For example, in Britain the primary function of the allowance is to compensate for the carer's loss of earnings, whereas in Michigan it is a means of rationalising the community care of poor people. In Finland the allowance for children's home care, and to a lesser extent the allowance for the home care of the elderly, disabled and the chronically ill, is intended as a compensation for not using communally organized services. In Finland the ideology of financially supporting informal care is grounded in the notion of the priority of public services, which is internationally quite exceptionally and which contradicts the principle of subsidiarity. Direct payment to the patient is a common alternative to carer's allowance.

Slater, P. (1995) 'Social work in Russia and the United Kingdom: a genuine exchange model', *Social Work in Europe* 2(1): 28-29.

Paper presented at a conference held in Moscow in 1994, drawing upon personal experience of an inter-country exchange programme.

Soisson, R. (1993) *Policymaking, research and staff training in residential care - Report of the 39th International Congress of FICE*, Zurich: FICE.

Collection of papers presented at the 39th FICE Congress by speakers from a wide range of countries (some papers in French and German).

Soydan, H. (1995) 'A cross-cultural comparison of how social workers in Sweden and England assess a migrant family', *Scandinavian Journal of Social Welfare* 4 (2): 85-93.

This article presents vignette data showing that social workers in Leicester, England and in Örebro, Sweden make different assessments when they are confronted by information about an immigrant family. One leading feature of the data is that all the respondents in Leicester immediately think that the information about the situation or the family might be false or malicious just because the family are immigrants. Another leading feature of the data is that a majority of social workers in Örebro consider the information to be correct. Many of these social workers relate the problem to the family's cultural background. The empirical data are interpreted with concepts borrowed from the fields of culture and organisation research, respectively.

Soyden, H. and Stal, R. (1994) 'How to use the Vignette technique in cross-cultural social work research', *Scandinavian Journal of Social Welfare* 3(2): 75-80.

In this article discusses the major premises of using the vignette technique in cross-cultural comparative social researcher discussed. In total, 247 vignettes were collected, 165 in Örebro, Sweden and 82 in the United Kingdom (73 in Leicester, England and 9 in the rural areas of Bangor, Wales). The vignettes were filled in by social workers working in the sector of child and family care. Since this technique is seldom used in cross-cultural comparative studies, it was necessary to develop a model for interpreting cross-cultural data. In this article, we consider methodological and practical aspects of the method adapted for cross-cultural social work research. A preliminary survey of our empirical data demonstrates the usefulness of such a model in understanding cross-cultural data. However, the empirical data will be presented in a later article.

Sykes, R and Alcock, P. (1998) *Developments in European Social Policy*, Bristol: The Policy Press.

Europe is undergoing fundamental shifts in its economic, political and social structures, and this forms the context for significant changes in social and other public policies. This text describes and analyses some of these changes and discusses the patterns of both convergence and divergence in the late 1990's.

Trevillion, S. (1997) 'The globalisation of European social work', *Social Work in Europe* 4(1): 1-9.

Throughout the post-war period, European social work has been strongly influenced by 'global' processes, but as the nature of these processes has changed, so too has their impact on European social work and European social workers. In this article, it is suggested that globalisation is not only reducing the resources available for social work and reshaping social work organisations, but that it is also creating new patterns of work and accountability and profoundly reshaping the fundamental values and philosophies upon which modern European social work has been built.

Trevillion, S. (1996) 'Towards a comparative analysis of collaboration', *Social Work in Europe* 3(1): 11-18.

This article explores the ways in which we currently talk about the 'problem of collaboration' in the UK and argues that our approaches are both intellectually and politically flawed and too narrow to be useful. It suggests that a broader comparative European perspective would create a more adequate account of the 'problem of collaboration', linking it to questions about how it is that we should respond to individual need whilst pursuing the goals of social inclusiveness. It is suggested this should form the basis of the long-awaited transformation of social work itself into a collaborative profession.

Üwen, E. (ed.) (1986) *Comparing Welfare States and Their Futures*, Aldershot: Gower.

Walden, T., Wolock, I. and Demone, H. W. (1990) 'Ethical decision making in human services: a comparative study', *Families in Society* 71 (1): 67-75.

Washington, Y. I. (1997) 'The role of social work in social exclusion', *Social Work in Europe* 4(3): 14-19.

Addresses the emerging concept of social exclusion as a focus for social work professional practice and argues that the diversity of social work activities means that the profession is best placed to respond.

Whitmore, E. and Wilson, M. (1997) 'Accompanying the process: social work and international development practice', *International Social Work* 40 (1): 57-74.

Williams, C. (1996) ' ERASMUS and SOCRATES in Koblenz: An alternative view', *Social Work in Europe* 3(3): 29-33.

Reflecting on the ERASMUS Evaluation Conference held in Koblenz in July 1996 when over 200 delegates came from all over Europe to report on and hear national perceptions of the scheme, some very obvious connections can be made with a major deficiency of the scheme's operation as a whole - that of attention to equal opportunities.

Wilson, V. (1989) *Primary Prevention of Substance Misuse in the youth services In Norway*, Caerphilly: Youth Link.

Reports on a Council of Europe Fellowship Study which looked at similarities and differences in control policies and primary prevention services and attitudes between Norway and Wales.

Single country studies

Children and families

Andersson, G. (1993) 'Support and relief: the Swedish contact person and contact family program', *Scandinavian Journal of Social Welfare* 2(2): 54-62.

> The Social Services Act in Sweden allows people with children to be offered a contact person or a contact family to provide help and support in personal matters or in matters concerning children. This legally regulated intervention is very much liked and the demand has increased year by year. Nothing in other countries quite corresponds to it. Virtually no research has been carried out on this, however, and systematic knowledge of how the intervention is used has been lacking. This article focuses on the application of the intervention to families with young children (0-3) and how social welfare inspectors and contact families evaluate it.

Backe-Hansen, E. (1994) 'Contact between young children in long-term care and their parents', *Scandinavian Journal of Social Welfare* 3(1): 24-30.

> In this article, the patterns of contact arrangements over time in a sample of Norwegian children in long-term care are analysed. General legal and professional thinking about the importance of continuity for children in care is contrasted with a view of contact arrangements as multifaceted and depending on other considerations than strictly professional ones. Maintaining contact is instead seen as ongoing negotiations between parents, workers, foster parents and children, with the parents as the weakest party. The variation inherent in the process of maintaining contact presupposes the use of discretion in the individual case. On the other hand, professional thinking about the importance of continuity needs to be translated into functional practice guidelines to aid the workers and to stimulate the development of arrangements that are more generally applicable.

Back-Wiklund, M. (1997) 'Children and family: a social work research programme', *Social Work in Europe* 4(2): 19-26.

> A Swedish research programme in the specialised areas of parenting and childhood in modern family cultures is presented, drawing on some of the results that have emerged as well as current planned projects.

Banks, N. J. (1994) 'Child abuse intervention in Milan', *Social Work in Europe* 1(3): 50-53.

Brief notes on the child protection system in Milan, and the role of family therapy, the courts, the image of social workers, and procedural differences throughout Italy.

Braduviciene I. et al. (1998) 'Developing fostering services in Lithuania' *Adoption and Fostering* 21(4): 14-22.

In this article, the social work team from a pilot Lithuanian fostering project in the city of Kaunas summarise their aims and progress in the context of local and national needs for child care services.

Browning, C. J. (1994) 'Public and private-sector out-of-home care in Denmark', *Social Service Review* 68(1): 20-32.

This study aims to discover why Danes make little use of resources from the private sector in what has been represented as a model child-care programme. With their welfare system under mounting strain at the same time tax money is being curtailed, special attention is paid to the expensive out-of-home placement practices common to local child-welfare operations. There is now token experimentation with kith - as alternatives to traditional child care institutions and foster homes - but resistance to placements in the households of extended families continues. Welfare administrators and politicians yield to the judgement and the decisions of a professional system dominated by social caseworkers.

Butler, A. C. (1995) 'The impact of social welfare policies on self-initiative and family structure: the case of Poland', *Social Service Review* 69(1): 1-30.

Over the past several decades, social welfare policy (broadly defined) has developed into a comprehensive system, creating the potential for unintended negative consequences as well as intended benefits. This article examines the extent to which the Polish experience is consistent with controversial hypothesis concerning the impact of social welfare policies on individual initiative and family structure. The abrupt changes currently taking place in Poland during the transition to a market economy provide an opportunity for us to observe the extent to which previous state policies have reduced individual initiative. Trends in divorce and out-of-wedlock childbearing are examined for evidence of weakening family structure.

Cervi, B. (1989) 'Where family comes first', *Community Care* 887: 16-18.

Department of Health (1988) *Protecting Children A Guide for Social Workers Undertaking a Comprehensive Assessment,* London: HMSO.

De Paul, J., and Arruabarrena, I. (1995) 'Behavior problems in school-aged physically abused and neglected children in Spain', *Child Abuse and Neglect* 19(4): 409-418.

Investigates behaviour problems in school-aged physically abused, neglected, and comparison children in the Basque Country (Spain). Follow- up analysis indicated that both abused and neglected children present more social problems, aggressive behaviour and lower school adjustment than the comparison children. Possible explanations of the findings are discussed and their implications for research and treatment are considered.

Egelund, T. (1998) 'More of the same: new rules for child protection in Denmark', *Nordisk Sosialt Arbeid* 18(4): 201-210.

Discusses the background to child protection in Denmark and argues that it is based on out of date premises.

Ekberg, K and Mjaavatn (eds) (1993) *Children at Risk: Proceedings,* Trondheim: The Norwegian Centre for Child Research.

Eriksen, J. (1994) 'Day care and the integration of disabled children in Norway', *Family Matters* 39: 20-25.

More than 40 per cent of all children in Norway under seven years of age participate in formal day care. The Norwegian Child Day Care Centre Act (1975) has ensured that it is a priority right of disabled children to have a place in mainstream care, and it applies to a wide range of disabilities including physical, intellectual, learning and behavioural. Discusses how the Norwegian day care system has allowed for the inclusion of disabled children.

Findlay, C. (1987-1988) 'Child abuse: the Dutch response', *Practice* 1(4): 374-381.

Gammon, E.A. and Dziegielewska, J. (1995) 'The butterflies of ARKA: grassroots initiatives for child welfare in Poland', *International Social Work* 38(2): 133-137.

In the transition from communist to democratic government the people of Poland must learn to deal at a community level with problems formerly addressed by centralized, bureaucratic institutions. The authors examine the ways in which one group of citizens covertly established a program to assist poor and disabled children and, in doing so, modelled the organisational skills needed to address other societal concerns. A brief outline is then given of the current efforts at community organisation being encouraged by government, the social work profession and non-profit agencies.

Geelen, H., van Unen, A. and Walraven, G. (1994) *Services integration for children and youth at risk in the Netherlands*, The Hague: Sardes.

Maps and describes the range of integrated services provision existing In the Netherlands for children and youth at risk, as part of the country-by- country OECD report series.

Greenfield, J. (1995) 'Inter-country adoption: a French perspective', *Social Work in Europe* 2(1): 41-43.

Considers the French experience of inter-country adoption.

Grevot, A. (1995) 'French Chronicle: The rise of ethical concerns in social work', *Social Work in Europe* 2(2): 23-24.

Reports on growing recognition in France for a common reference point for the various professionals involved in child welfare and protection.

Grevot, A. (1998) 'Abused childhood': child maltreatment - a major national crusade', *Social Work in Europe* 5(3): 46-47.

Describes how in France the government initiated a national campaign for the 'protection of abused children' with the slogan 'if everyone moves, it will move'. The objectives were, on one hand, to mobilise the professionals and volunteers of all sectors and, on the other, to raise the awareness of all French citizens to child abuse. Describes the objectives and the impact of the campaign.

Harwin, J. (1988) 'Learning from the USSR', *Social Work Today* (8 September): 18-19.

The child care debate in Russia revolves around how best to improve the quality of care for children without parents.

Harwin, J. (1992) 'Adoption policy and practice in Russia', *Adoption and Fostering* 16(1): 16-22.

Hay Jones, D. (1991) 'Scandal in Scandinavia', *Community Care* 879:12-4

More then ten years after it was made illegal in Sweden for parents to hit their children a child abuse case has hit the national headlines.

Hetherington, R. and Sprangers, A. (1994) 'The work of the Flemish Mediation Commission', *Social Work in Europe* 1(2): 50-54.

A brief description of the Flemish Mediation Commission and the child protection system in Belgium, followed by an interview with a member of the Commission.

Hill, M. and Cairns-Smith, D. A. (1995) 'Developing a child care management training course for Romania', *Social Work in Europe* 2(1): 20-27.

Describes the context of child care services in Romania, general economic and social conditions, child care and social work services past and present, the development of links with Scotland, principles and elements of a one year course, implementation, feedback, and future developments.

Humphrey, M. and Humphrey, H. (1993) *Inter-Country Adoption: Practical Accounts,* London: Routledge.

Johnson, A.K. et al. (1993) 'Foster care and adoption policy on Romania: suggestions for international intervention', *Child Welfare* 72(5): 489-506.

Building an effective child welfare system is a monumental task facing post-revolution Romania. Following revelations on American and Western European television about the large number of 'orphans' in Romania, many couples flocked to that country to adopt children. A significant number of adopted Romanian children were brought to the United States. Some of these children are now evidencing problems that are bringing them to the attention of health and social service agencies. This article examines the macroeconomic policies that led to the institution-alistion of a large number of children in Romania. Although institutional care is the current norm, a legal basis exists for building family foster care as an alternative. Romania's new adoption law replaces private adoptions with agency-based work. International adoption agencies are involved in developing community-based foster-care and permanency planning as part of their work. This article challenges international adoption agencies to use clinical assessments of developmental delays and more rigorous health examinations for children released for adoption.

Johnson, I. M., Sigler, R. T. and Crowley, J. E. (1994) 'Domestic violence: a comparative study of perceptions and attitudes toward domestic abuse cases among social service and criminal justice professionals', *Journal of Criminal Justice* 22(3): 237-48.

Jonker, F. and Jonker-Bakker, P. (1991) 'Experiences with ritualist child sexual abuse: a case study from the Netherlands', *Child Abuse and Neglect* 15(3): 191-196.

> Describes allegations of large-scale ritual abuse, the reactions of the police, parents and the local community and proposes improvements to assessment methods.

Kemecsei, E. (1996) 'The family under the impact of change in Hungary', *Social Work in Europe* 2(1): 30-35.

> Extracts from a paper presented at the inaugural symposium of a conference on 'The Changing Family in Europe', organised by Bournmouth University and the Fachhochschule of Niederhein Krefeld Monchengladbach.

King, M. (1995) 'Connecting with the French connection', *Social Work in Europe* 2(1): 6-40.

> Following the publication of 'Child Protection: a View from Abroad', considers the need, when analysing the French 'juge des enfants' system, for a careful analysis of French society and culture, including political ideology and the role of law and the courts to throw light upon the fundamental differences of structure, practice, belief and attitude to the British system.

Korintus, M. (1994) 'Childcare in Hungary', *Concern* 88(Spring): 4-5.

> Looks at the childcare system for children under three in Hungary. State support for mothers is relatively generous; however, the economic situation is driving more women into full-time employment. At the same time, the cost of providing childcare is an enormous burden on the state budget. The Social Act (1992) passed many of the state's responsibilities on to local authorities. The National Institute of Day Care Centres (BOMI) are working to make available a wider range of childcare services and to provide training and guidelines for services.

Lemierre, R. (1994) 'Juvenile Services of the French Justice Ministry', *Social Work in Europe* 1(2): 42-47.

> Describes, with flow charts, the different levels of administrative power in France, the place of the Juvenile Judicial Protection

Service with the Ministry of Justice, the process of dealing with minors in dangers or at risk, procedure following arrest of young people.

Lier, L. (1997) 'The Copenhagen model of early preventive intervention aimed at high risk families', *Social Work in Europe* 4(2): 15-18.

Describes the development of infant psychiatric services in Copenhagen, aimed at high-risk families, primarily mothers with mental illness and their children from 0-3 years old.

McPhatter, A. R. (1997) 'Cultural competence in child welfare: what is it? How do we achieve it? What happens without it?', *Child Welfare* 76(1): 255-78.

Claims that provision of culturally relevant, effective medical and psychosocial services is yet to be achieved. Asserts that before significant progress toward these goals can be made, what constitutes cultural competence must be elucidated. Describes the Cultural Competence Attainment Model and addresses the effects of cultural incompetence.

Miguel, A., et al. (1995) 'The maltreatment of intellectually handicapped children and adolescents', *Child Abuse and Neglect* 19(2): 205-215.

A questionnaire specifically designed to detect and discover the prevalence of maltreatment in a sample of children with learning difficulties in Castilla-Leon, Spain revealed that eleven and a half percent of these children were subjected to maltreatment, with physical neglect being the most frequent. It was also discovered that problems between the child's parents, the child's behaviour and the interaction between both aspects were significant factors in situations of maltreatment.

Mitchell, J. and Gelloz, N. (1997) 'Supporting families and strengthening communities: the role of the 'specialised prevention' movement in France', *Social Work in Europe* 4(3): 2-11.

Looks at how a collective approach to prevention is commonplace in the French system, where social policies stress the importance of intervening to promote solidarity between the members of local communities. Describes one such initiative, known as specialised prevention.

Nakou, S. And Stefanos, P. (1996) *The Child in the World of Tomorrow: The Next Generation*, Oxford: Pergamon.

Nijnatten C.V. (1988) 'Case planning in the Netherlands', *Child Welfare* LXVII (5): 4O3-41O.

Nissen, M. (1996) 'Concepts of work in social work - professional help, volunteers, and life in local culture projects', *Nordisk Sosialt Arbeid* 16(4): .266-282.

Based on experience from Sjakket, a Copenhagen development project helping 'street kids', fundamental discursive forms structuring relations between work and life in social work are discussed. In the narrative of one young women growing from alcohol abuse and homelessness to the status of a 'resource person' in Sjakket's mutual help organisation, we trace the ability of the project to meet the kids on their own terms and to engage them in participation. The discursive form, paraphrased as "Help is self- help in the community", realised in practical project life allows for a flexible generalisation of action possibilities that remain in close contact with personal peculiarities and grow in immediate friendships, but never-the-less reach the level of universalism distinguishing the welfare state. The idea is that this results from the open-ended cultural and political reproduction of the local culture materialised in the project and its co-operation with democratic municipal agencies.

Philpot, T. (1991) 'Crime and punishment', *Community Care* (24 November): 12-14.

The Dutch child protection system eschews recourse to law in favour of treatment for abusers and their families.

Poulsen, A. (1995) 'The Danish agenda for children and young people in need', *Children UK* 4(Spring): 3.

Describes a new Danish action plan for children and young people who most need support.

Redding, D. (1990) 'Discovering the neglected', *Community Care*, (825): 20-22.

Looks at the low levels of care in Romanian institutions that have come to light following the revolution.

Reich, D. (1990) 'Children of the nightmare', *Adoption and Fostering* 14(3): 9-14.

Reviews the background to the abandoned children in Romania and the problems of adopting such a child.

Reitan, T.C. (1997) 'Getting a head start: early provision of day care among municipalities in Norway', *Scandinavian Journal of Social Welfare* 6(4): 268-278.

Focusing on the relationship between environmental inputs and policy outcomes, this article attempts to identify characteristics influencing the propensity towards early child care provision in Norway. The persisting importance of gender-specific variables is discussed, suggesting different interpretations of the results in relation to the feminisation of politics.

Ross, S. (1987) *Systems Intervention in Child Care: The Implications of Gregory Bateson's Theories of Systems Change for Planning and Providing Social Work Services for Children and Families in Trouble,* Unpublished PhD Theses, University of Keele.

This thesis traces the development of the modern cybernetic systems movement and examines its impact on the social sciences. In particular it focuses on the work of Gregory Bateson the biologist, anthropologist, philosopher and cyberneticist whose research, from the 1950s to 1980 when he died, into the ways systems change, develop, and adapt over time underpins much of the practice of family therapy in Europe and the United States at the present time.

Sariola, H. And Uutela, A. (1992) 'The prevalence and context of family violence against children in Finland', *Child Abuse and Neglect* 16: 823-832.

The prevalence and context of violence against children in their families was surveyed as part of a study on the sexual abuse of children. A random sample of 409 comprehensive school classes with approximately 9,000 15-year-olds was asked to fill out questionnaires anonymously. Findings include: the highest incidence of severe violence was found amongst youth living in families with a stepfather, unemployment tended to increase incidence, violence was reported least by farming families or Swedish- speaking families. Overall, the frequency of violence towards children in Finland is significantly lower than in the U.S. Comparison with Sweden seems to show an identical level of child abuse.

Slette, S., Hagen, G., and Maier, H.W. (1993) 'Permanency planning principles in the Norwegian child welfare system and their application to practice', *Child Welfare* 71(1): 77-88.

Offers a translation of the ten basic principles that guide Norwegian child welfare practice.

Solomon, R. (1994) 'East meets West: a community fostering service in Warsaw', *Social Work in Europe* 1(1): 11-20.

The author describes his experience of being invited to advise on the establishment of community fostering project in Warsaw, and what he learnt from the Polish residential child care system, and the model developed.

Spriggs, A. (1994) 'What's in a name? A guide to the French social worker in child and family services', *Social Work in Europe* 1(2): 48-49.

Brief notes on the meanings, roles and positions of the various professional titles that come under the umbrella 'travailleur social/sociale' title in France.

Stelmaszuk, Z. W. (1994) 'Fostering in Poland', *Social Work in Europe* 1(2): 39-41.

Reviews the long history of fostering in Poland, and recent developments.

Stevenson, O. (ed.) (1989) *Child Abuse: Public Policy and Professional Practice,* London: Harvester Wheatsheaf.

Syzmanski, L. S., and Seppala, H. T. (1995) 'Specialized family care for children with developmental disabilities: the Finnish experience', *Child Welfare* 74(2): 367-381.

This article describes features of Finland's specialized family care for children with disabilities, including professionalization and training of foster parents and the establishment of municipal employee-like status for them, long-term placements, and the preservation of relationships with biological families whenever possible. A case example of a 12-year old child with mental retardation and autistic disorder who is in specialized care is included.

Textor, M. (1990) 'Helping multi-problem families in West Germany: a new approach to social work', *Practice* 4(1): 56-62.

Textor, M. (1992) 'Adoptions in West Germany: attitudes of social workers', *British Journal of Social Work* 22(5): 551-64.

Textor, M. (1995) 'Youth and family service welfare in Germany', *International Social Work* 38(4): 379-386.

After a short overview of social changes in Germany, a new law, the Child Welfare Law of 1991, is presented. Its principles and rationale as well as the areas covered are described. All the different child and related family services are not mentioned. Moreover, related services not covered by the law are described. Thus, an overview is given of a very large part of the German welfare system. It shows that this is a very complex and diverse system making it difficult for clients to orientate themselves. In conclusion therefore, the need to connect the different services is underlined.

Thomas, N. (1994) 'Child welfare services in Russia', *Children and Society* 8(4): 327-332.

This is an account of a visit to Moscow in May 1994 to assess the possibilities for collaboration in developing child welfare services in Russia. The authors argue that the present situation is a critical one for millions of children, and that there is an urgent need for practical and theoretical assistance from Britain.

Todorova, V. (1996) 'Parents, children and child protection under Bulgarian law', *Social Work in Europe* 3(3): 53-56.

Describes Bulgarian legislation of the family and the child which is based on three principles: firstly, that children must be brought up in the family of their own parents: secondly, that the state and society in general must provide assistance to parents in bringing up children. The third principle gives parents certain guarantees that their parental rights and obligations in respect of the first two principles will be observed and respected.

Van Wel, F. (1992) 'A century of families under supervision in the Netherlands', *British Journal of Social Work* 22(2): 147-166.

Reviews twentieth century attitudes, policies and practice in working with families with serious problems and argues that interactions were based on an amalgam of rational and fictional elements in the underlying theories.

Virtanen, P. (1994) *Services Integration for Children and Youth at Risk and Their Families* Helsinki: National Research and Development Centre for Welfare and Health.

Vorria, P. (1995) 'The changing social profile of mothers whose children are admitted into institutional care in Greece', *Scandinavian Journal of Social Welfare* 4(1): 36-43.

Reports research into the social profile of mothers in Greece who had children admitted to institutional care - one group whose children were aged 2.5.-5.5 years at the time, and one group whose children were aged 15.5-17.5 years at the time. Comparison with control groups was made, which found that study mothers in both groups were from a lower social class, had experienced more adversity in childhood, and had more health problems. They had left their parental homes and given birth at a young age and faced more difficulties (financial, housing, marital). The older group of study mothers more often had their children admitted into care because of financial difficulties or illegitimacy, in contrast with the younger mothers who more often gave the reason of marital breakdown.

Wallace, C. (1995) 'Young people and families in Poland: changing times, changing dependencies?', *Journal of European Social Policy* 5(2): 97-109.

Considers the relationships between parents and children in Polish families in the situation of social transformation. Two main hypotheses are considered: whether the strong family bonds developed under the communist regime are weakening with the new economic conditions and whether there is a process of 'individualization' as in many other western countries with young people seeking greater autonomy and independence from family ties. The paper concludes that although there is some evidence of a move towards individualization and a changing relationship between parents and children, there are nevertheless ore continuities in family relationships because of the continuing economic problems in which people find themselves and the lack of improvement or even worsening of many of the conditions which encourage close family ties in the first place. Family obligations and ties of loyalty and duty continue to exert a strong influence.

Disability (physical and learning)

Brandon, D., et al. (1998) 'Romania: legislation and provision of services for people with a mental handicap', *Social Work in Europe* 5(2): 55-58.

Looks at the experience of parents, carers and workers in accessing and understanding current legislation for people with a mental handicap in Romania.

Farmer, R., Rohde J. and Sacks B. (1992) *Changing Services for People with Learning Disabilities*, London: Chapman and Hall.

Describes the history of provision of services for people with learning disabilities, and the setting up of a register by the NW

Thames Regional Health Authority to aid in the long term planning of services. Goes on to make a comparative study of places of residence and the people living there, including family homes, hospitals, private or voluntary residential care, local authority care, and NHS hostels. Goes on to discuss the findings of this study and make recommendations.

Gammon, E. A. and Dzlegielewska, J. (1997) 'Polish social services to families of children with disabilities: practice in an emerging setting', *International Social Work* 40(4): 393-406.

Discusses a pilot study of the roles that social workers in Poland perform as they attempt to assist families whose children have disabilities. Barriers to service provision were examined, as were the cultural, economic and political frameworks in which those services are provided. Results demonstrate the emergence of a dynamic group of workers interested in clarifying the mission of their profession and in educating the public about the services it can provide to families.

Hollander, A. (1993) 'Rights to special services for people with developmental disabilities in Sweden - the risk and benefits of a legislative approach', *Scandinavian Journal of Social Welfare* 2(2): 63-68.

Several major pieces of legislation in Sweden have been developed and enacted during the twentieth century to enable people with disabilities to live as normal a life as possible. The legal instrument is not supposed to depend on political economic trends. Important changes in the new Act on Social Services for Developmentally Disabled Persons from 1986 include qualitative demands and the right to self-determination for those individuals. The special services covered by the law are called social rights. The implementation of these rights is under the jurisdiction of politically appointed councils in counties or municipalities. The decisions made by these authorities can be appealed in administrative courts. Judicial review is supposed to be an instrument for the protection of citizens from the authorities responsible for services. In theory, at least, when one disabled person wins a case in court, the precedent should trickle down to all individuals in similar predicaments. But this does not always occur. One problem is that the law has no sanctions to force local authorities to follow the precedents or to execute court decisions. This article focuses on the Act and on the interplay between court cases and precedents and the decisions made by local authorities.

Johansson, S. et al. (1993) 'Do public services influence patterns of informal care? Informal networks and public home care in three Swedish municipalities', *Scandinavian Journal of Social Welfare* 2(2): 69-79.

Whether an individual receives home care services depends on two factors: the functional disability of the care recipient and the caregiver's gender, when the living arrangements of the care recipient are controlled. Data from a longitudinal study of social networks and home care organisation in three municipalities in Sweden show that care recipients with a severe disability receive more home care services than others. In cases where the main caregiver lives together with the care recipient, the public services are adjusted to the family situation and are independent of the functional disability of the care recipient. Care recipients who live with the primary caregiver receive less formal help than do care recipients who live alone. When the primary caregiver does not live together with the care recipient, the public services are adjusted to the functional disability of the care recipient and are independent of the primary caregiver's gender. Care recipients supported by a male helper received more formal help than care recipients supported by a female helper. Those supported by a female helper received more informal help. Various models of relationships, supplementation and complementation between informal care and public services are discussed. The dependence on public home services is high. Assistance with basic activities of daily living is the first area requiring complementary contributions from the public services. A special type of kin independence was found, related to the function of public services in a modern and gender-equal society. The results provoke a discussion on research design as well as comments on welfare policy and gender equality in the transformation of the welfare state.

Landau, R., Guttmann, D. and Talyigas, K. (1998) 'Eligibility criteria for cash assistance for older and disabled people in Hungary: a model for countries in passage from a planned to a market economy', *British Journal of Social Work* 28(2): 233-246.

Discusses how the political and economic changes presently taking place in the Central and Eastern European countries are accompanied by profound social changes which impact hardest on the well-being of older and disabled people. Based on the experience of a Hungarian non-governmental social agency, a model for eligibility criteria for cash assistance for vulnerable peoples is suggested.

McLaughlin, E. (1992) *Paying for Care in Europe: A Study of Carer's Income Needs and the Invalid care Allowance in Britain. Proceedings of a Conference on Informal Care in Europe,* University of York: Social Policy Research Unit.

Mental health

Ardenghi, M. (1995) 'Beyond the asylum', *Social Work in Europe*, 2(2): 25-27.

A social worker/co-ordinator in one of the area psychiatric services in Bologna traces the developments which have occurred in her field over the last twenty-four years.

Asimopoulos, H. (1998) '"Reform", developments and prevailing trends in mental health care in Greece', *Social Work in Europe* 5(1): 41-48.

Provides an overview of recent changes to mental health care in Greece, and outlines how there are no developments towards adopting the model of community mental health care.

Blonde, D. (1995) Aspects of mental health in Belgium II: the role of the social worker', *Social Work in Europe* 2(2): 29-30.

Brief notes by a social worker and family therapist at the Psychiatric Crisis Intervention Centre at the University Hospital of Leuven.

Goodwin, S. (1989) 'Community care and the mentally ill in England and Wales: myths, assumptions and reality', *Journal of Social Policy* 18(1): 27-52.

It is widely recognised that there are many problems with the community care policy for the mentally ill, which has been in operation in England and Wales since the late 1950s. However, many existing accounts of the development of the policy rest upon a variety of erroneous assumptions about how it has evolved, and which in turn affect our understanding of how it might be changed. Some of these assumptions are examined, and it is argued that frequently they fail to acknowledge how both the rhetoric and the reality of the policy have developed. Taking this critique into account, a more accurate assessment of how to understand community care for the mentally ill is offered.

Hansson, J-H. (1993) 'To be or to be trained to be - on emerging and diverging ideological traditions in organising day care activities for people with severe mental disorders in Sweden', *Scandinavian Journal of Social Welfare* 2(2): 80-87.

Organised activities for people with severe mental disorders have until recently been the societal task of one human service organisation, the medical speciality of psychiatry. With former psychiatric inpatients moving out into the local community and with heavier dependence on outpatient poly-clinic care, the situation is slowly changing. Day care activities for people with severe mental disorder are organised with an increasing involvement of the social services. The aim of this article is, using data from a national survey carried out in 1991 in Sweden, to describe and categorise how day care units interpret their tasks. Results show that claims-making activities still adhere largely to a therapeutic paradigm in spite of the outspoken social character of the work of organising everyday life activities.

Hansson, J-H., Tengvald, K. (1993) 'No longer a one-man job? On day activities in mental health care in Sweden', *Scandinavian Journal of Social Welfare* 2(4): 186-196.

Swedish psychiatry is organisationally in line with the international development of closing down old large mental hospitals. As in other countries, problems of provision of care for severely mentally ill people can be observed. An organisationally new field focusing on the activities of daily living is developing, however. This was surveyed nationally in Spring 1991 and parts of these results are presented and discussed. The field is characterized by profound uncertainty manifested in the fact that psychiatry is no longer doing the work alone. Local social services take on a growing responsibility trying to make claims on how to define the work even if psychiatry is dominant, both in organisational and discursive power. Promising characteristics in joint venture units set up between psychiatry and local social services opens up for discussions on who, in what ways and with what means these new forms of care are going to be pursued.

Huggins, T. et al. (1997) 'How to adjust the institution to the child', *Social Work in Europe* 4(2): 42-45.

Presents an example of how a child psychiatric institution in Norway can adjust to the needs of children. Highlights the qualities and attitudes that are vital to the atmosphere in which the therapeutic process can take place.

Lier, L. (1997) 'The Copenhagen model of early preventative intervention aimed at high risk families', *Social Work in Europe* 4(2): 15-18.

Describes the development of psychiatric services for infants in Copenhagen, aimed at high-risk families, primarily mothers with mental illness and their children from 0-3 years old.

Mapp, S. (1994) 'Sun, sea and social work', *Community Care*, 1042: 28-29.

A mobile unit of social workers in Greece is saving villagers the trauma of being sent to psychiatric hospitals in the cities. The unit's social workers effectively become psychiatric social workers through in-service supervision, and must go through psychoanalysis as part of their training. Describes the work of the unit.

Meier, C. and Rezzonico, G. (1994) 'Care in place at the Centro al Dragonato', *Care in Place*, 1(1): 9-26.

Describes the work of a day centre in the Swiss Canton of Ticino for people with mental health problems.

Steeno, M. (1995) 'Aspects of Mental Health Services in Belgium I: the development of services', *Social Work in Europe* 2(2): 27-28.

Reflects on twenty years experience as a social worker in the psychiatric team at the University Psychiatric Clinic 'Salve Mater' at Lovenjoel near Leuven.

Zavirsek, D. and Flaker, V. (1995) 'Developing culturally sensitive mental health services in Slovenia', *Social Work in Europe* 2(2): 30-36.

Examines the issue of culture in the process of changing mental health processes. Firstly, the specificity's of the Slovene mental health system and its institutional peculiarities are considered, and ideas about the desired constituents of a culturally sensitive programme.

Offenders

Baldry, A. C. (1998) 'Victim-offender mediation in the Italian juvenile justice system: the role of the social worker', *British Journal of Social Work* 28(5): 729-44.

Mediation, according to the restorative justice approach, balances the victims' needs against holding offenders responsible for the harm caused and requiring them to make reparation for it. Victim-offender mediation in the Italian juvenile justice system is not, as yet, widely implemented. Social workers, employed by the

Juvenile Criminal Justice Department, are the only professionals involved in mediation. Results from an Italian survey conducted with social workers, who are responsible for victim-offender mediation as part of their probation duties, show that mediation programmes remain limited and unstructured. A case study is reported which shows, moreover, that mediation can be successfully undertaken even with serious offences and that both the victim and the offender can benefit from it. Issues related to the implications and social policy impact of mediation as a social work practice are also considered.

Barberan, J.M. (1996) 'Mediation in Spanish youth justice', *Social Work in Europe* 3(3): 36-38.

Discusses the impact of new legislation introduced in 1992 on mediation programmes for young offenders in Spain.

Ciufu, D. (1997) 'Reforming Romanian youth justice', *Social Work in Europe* 4(2): 52-55.

Provides a background to reforming the youth justice system in Romania.

Dixon, L. (1995) 'Mainland European women in Holloway prison', *Social Work in Europe* 2(3): 57-59.

A prison based probation officer working in Holloway prison discusses the way in which the British Criminal Justice System impacts upon women from foreign countries. She also recounts her experience of organising a Foreign Nationals Day in Holloway prison to raise consciousness amongst staff and the voluntary and statutory groups involved. Two case histories are used to illustrate the range of problems involved.

Poulopoulos, C. and Tsiboukli, A. (1998) 'The origins and evolution of Greek therapeutic communities for drug addicts', *Social Work in Europe* 5(2): 29-33.

This article is concerned with the origins and development of therapeutic communities in Greece. The evolution of American and other European therapeutic communities is described and emphasis is placed on the differences in the ways in which these communities developed and influenced the generation of therapeutic communities in Greece.

Ravenscroft, L. (1997) 'The Norwegian criminal justice system: report of a study tour', *Social Work in Europe* 4(1): 43.

Under the auspices of the Overseas Committee of the Judicial

Studies Board, twenty magistrates from all over England and Wales spent five days in Oslo at the beginning of June 1996, following a programme arranged by the Royal Ministry of Justice, visiting courts, prisons, probation projects, and a special drug-rehabilitation programme. This account is based on what was learned on this study tour.

Romano, C.A. (1997) 'The Italian social co-operative as a rehabilitative tool in work with ex-offenders', *Social Work in Europe* 4(1): 42-43.

Describes Italian Co-operatives which it is claimed are one of the few instruments which can translate the idea of work as rehabilitation into practice.

Spiess, G. (1994) 'Diverting away from custody, diverting away from trial - how far can we go? The German experience', *Social Work in Europe* 1(2): 28-38.

Extensive review of probation, sanctions and diversion in Germany, with statistics.

van der Laan, P.H. (1994) 'Day Training Centres for young offenders in the Netherlands: practices, perspectives and disappointments', *Social Work in Europe* 1(2): 17-23.

Reviews alternatives to custody in the Netherlands and the development of day training centres for juvenile offenders.

Older people

Alber, J. (1994) *The Debate over Long-term Care in Germany,* paper presented at the OECD Meeting on Caring for Frail Elderly People, Paris, OECD.

Alber, J. (1992) *Social and Economic Policies for Older People in Germany,* Brussels: Commission of the European Communities (Document V/5098/93DE).

Baars, J., Knipscheer, K., and Breebart, K. (1992) *The Impact of Social and Economic Policies on Older People in the Netherlands,* Amsterdam: Free University.

Bartlett, N. (1989) 'Caring, the French Way', *Community Care*, 788: 20-22.

Home care services for the elderly in France have been provided by non- profit-making organisations for 25 years. Service provision can vary between such organisations.

Berenbaum, R. J. (1997) 'Transfer of information from adult day care to nursing homes; bridging the gaps in the long term care of dementia patients', *Journal of Gerontological Social Work* 27(4): 85-95.

This paper proposes the use of a standard form to be sent to a nursing home by adult day care staff when a client with dementia stops attending adult day care and moves into an institution. It contains non-confidential information that the adult day care staff has learned about their client that can be useful to the institutional staff in their efforts to treat the new client as a unique person. The use of such a form will be beneficial for the client as well as the staff members of both adult day care and the institution and will fill a gap in the continuum of care.

Carroll, B. (1991) 'Developments in care for elderly people in Ireland', *Social Policy and Administration* 25(3): 238-248.

Daatland, S.O. (1992) 'Ideals lost? Current trends in Scandinavian welfare policies on ageing', *Journal of European Social Policy*, 2(1): 33-47.

Considers the extent to which the traditional ideals underlying the Scandinavian welfare state - solidaristic and egalitarian - are under threat in the light of signs of less state ambition, and public criticisms about the amount of public expenditure.

Department of Health (1989) *Caring for People: Community Care in the Next Decade and Beyond,* London: HMSO

Dieck, M. (1994) 'Reforming against the grain: long-term care in Germany' in Page, R. and Baldock, J., *Social Policy Review 6,* London: Social Policy Association.

Driest, P. F. (1988) 'Social services and the elderly in the Netherlands', *Journal of Gerontological Social Work* 12(1-2): 153-66.

The 'greying' of the population of the Netherlands is a slow, but persistent phenomena, that started at the turn of this century and will accelerate in its last 25 years as a result of decreasing number of births along with an increasing average life expectancy. Two features in this greying are remarkable: the proportions of the very aged and of women. Women account for nearly 60% of those 65 and over and two thirds of the 80 and over population.

Evers, A. and Olk, T. (1991) 'The mix of care provisions for the frail elderly in the Federal Republic of Germany. Deficits, changes and prospects of reform', Vienna: *Eurosocial Report* 40(3): 59-100.

Evers et al. Payments for Care: A Comparative Overview, Aldershot: Avebury.

Includes chapters on: Austria, Federal Republic of Germany Hungary, Norway, Slovenia, Sweden, United Kingdom

Falkingham, J. (1989) 'Dependency and ageing in Britain: a re-examination of the evidence', *Journal of Social Policy* 18(2): 211-233.

There has been growing concern over the consequences for public expenditure of an increasing number of elderly people dependent on a relatively diminishing working population. This concern stems largely from demographically determined dependency ratios and it is not necessarily the case that a change in the age profile of the population will lead to a greater burden of dependency. The 'engine of dependency' is shown to have at least two other cylinders - patterns of labour-force participation across age and gender, and levels of unemployment. Policy to date has had surprisingly narrow focus in view of the dual role of economic and demographic forces in influencing the ratio of dependency. The economic and political feasibility of alternative policy options is discussed.

Family Policy Studies Centre (1991) *An Ageing Population, London:* Help the Aged.

Florea, A., Colombini, L., Costanzo, A. and Cuneo, A. (1992) *Social and Economic Policies for Older People in Italy*, Milan: ISTISSS.

Hartl, J., Kasalova, H. and Sandera, J. (1991) 'Social policy, social care and the case of the elderly in Czechoslovakia. An outline of past trends and future prospects' in Evers, A. and Svetlik, I. (eds) *New Welfare Mixes in Care for the Elderly*, Vienna: Eurosocial Report 40(1)

Jansen, B. (1995) 'Abuse of the elderly in the Netherlands: policy and experience of combating abuse of the elderly', *Social Work in Europe*, 2(3): 18-24.

In 1988, the government of the Netherlands conducted an exploratory study into the abuse of the elderly. This gave rise to a series of activities, which are reviewed in this article. The article covers a survey conducted in 1988 into the mistreatment of elderly people living at home, in homes for the elderly and in nursing homes. National organisations and the general public were also surveyed to attempt to gauge the extent of elder abuse and an insight into the kinds of abuse among the elderly.

Psychological mistreatment and financial abuse were the types of abuse most frequently reported. The results of the survey led to the setting up of two experimental help-centres of the elderly which helped bring recognition to the problem of abuse of the elderly.

Johns, S. and Jukles, O. (1995) 'Norway: developing elder protective services', *Social Work in Europe* 2(3): 2-7.

Norwegians first became aware of the problem of elder abuse a decade ago. Government-supported research focused on why this particular problem has fallen outside the field of elder care, which otherwise is extensively developed in the welfare state. With Government support, it has been possible to apply social research to the design of a social work development project to find out the extent of elder abuse in Norway. The results of the research made it clear that elder abuse is a problem and that in spite of welfare, the victims do not receive the necessary help. Looks at implications for policy.

Johnson, P. and Falkingham, J. (1992) *Ageing and Economic Welfare,* London: Sage.

Korpi, W. (1995) 'The position of the elderly in the welfare state: comparative perspectives on old-age care in Sweden', *Social Service Review* 69(2): 242-273.

The 'graying of populations' in the advanced industrial countries has created increasing concerns among policy makers. In Sweden, the proportion of the aged has increased very fast. Because Sweden is known as an advanced welfare state, it is of interest to look at its efforts to deal with the problems of the aged. This article presents information on the economic, social and health situation of the elderly and discusses the development of institutional and home care for the elderly in Sweden. Where available, comparative data are used to place Sweden in an international perspective.

Lagergren, M. (1993) 'The residential home - what difference does it make? Comparing the public systems of care for the elderly and disabled in two Swedish municipalities', *Scandinavian Journal of Social Welfare* 2(1): 25-32.

Two municipalities in Sweden - Solna and Sigtuna - have taken part in a project (the ASIM project) aimed at developing a system for monitoring and analysing the public system of long-term care and assistance for elderly and disabled people. The two municipalities have chosen different alternatives in the question of residential homes. In Solna they have been retained and in Sigtuna they have been converted into sheltered housing. By separating the clients into different classes of dependence using the ASIM assessment, it is shown that in Solna, compared with Sigtuna, fewer of the most dependent clients are in long-term hospital care and fewer of the high-medium category are in domiciliary care. The data were used to calculate the distribution of clients and the average dependence on the different levels of care if Solna were to apply the care pattern of Sigtuna and vice versa.

Le Dain, Y. (1995) 'French connections for ageing interactively', *Ageing International* 22(1): 36-38.

Reports on the French Minitel system, which offers the older population of France the opportunity to electronically network and obtain information.

Lucchetti, M. (1995) 'The families of the elderly in Italy', *Ageing International* 22(4): 47-50.

Few data are needed to get a clear picture of the demographic changes taking place in Italy. The older population is increasing as is the proportion of women in this population. Among those 65-plus, there are 68 men to 100 women. The ratio of men to women is even lower among those 75- plus because women usually live longer. The article examines the implications of this for service providers and carers of the elderly.

Marineck, C. (1995) 'Changing Slovenia's delivery system', *Ageing International* 22(1): 45-46.

Brief notes on the provision of aids to older people in Slovenia.

Mayence, S. (1993) 'Older people in Charleroi', *Social Policy and Administration* 27(3): 221-234.

Reports on a study of older people in Charleroi, Belgium, and their views on neighbourhood life, family, dependency and domiciliary services, health, leisure-time and voluntary action, and retirement. One of a series of companion studies.

Monahan, D. J. (1993) 'Assessment of dementia patients and their families: an ecological family centred approach', *Health and Social Work* 18(2): 123-31.

Demand for assessment and treatment of dementia patients and their families is expected to increase substantially by the end of this decade, considering current estimates of about 4 million dementia patients. This article guides social work practice in the assessment of dementia patients and their families using an ecological-family-centred (EFC) model of practice. A case presentation illustrates how to apply the EFC model while incorporating ethnically sensitive practice principles. The model organises complex assessment issues that often arise when working with families of dementia patients and illustrates the significance of cultural diversity in case practice. Literature on families of dementia patients is reviewed, an intervention plan for the family system is outlined, and implications for practice are noted.

Noro, A. and Aro, S. (1996) 'Is home care a realistic alternative to residential care among institutionalized elderly people in Finland?' *Scandinavian Journal of Social Welfare* 5(4): 249-258.

The high rate of institutionalisation among elderly people in Finland is widely recognized among policy-makers. Studies how realistic the wishes for *deinstitutionalisation* are among the least sick elderly people in residential care, and what patient characteristics predict whether residential care is appropriate. This issue was assessed by the residential home personnel. Personnel assessment of institutional care as appropriate was mainly explained by patients' needing help with medication, limitations in activities of daily living, absence of own home return to, no living children, incontinence, and poor vision. Discharging elderly people from long-term residential care back to society is limited by factors such as inadequate housing and shortage of domiciliary care and rehabilitative services, as well as by attitudes among the institutionalised elderly people themselves. It seems more realistic to prevent the inappropriate institutionalisation of elderly people that to discharge the small numbers of fairly independent individuals already in residential homes.

Ochotorena, J. and Zugasti, J. L. L. (1995) 'Elder abuse in Spain', *Social Work in Europe* 2(3): 12-13.

For political reasons, Spain has been isolated from the rest of Europe for a number of years. This has resulted in slow progress of both welfare and the means to support social protection. It was not until the middle of the 1980s that Spain began to address subjects in relation to family violence. The article outlines how interest in, resources for, and research related to, elder abuse evolved in Spain.

Ogg, J. (1995) 'Elder abuse in France', *Social Work in Europe* 2(3): 8-11.

In France many health and social care practitioners are becoming aware that despite considerable economic resources directed towards health and social care provision for old age, there is a widening gap between those who receive an adequate or more than adequate level of services and those who are excluded. For those older people faced with disability or ill health, home and family will be their main source of support. A growth in unregulated private home-care by individuals and agencies means that this sector mostly consists of untrained and unqualified staff with no support. The possibility of abuse and exploitation in such circumstances therefore remains open.

O'Loughlin, A. (1995) 'Elder abuse: a perspective from Ireland', *Social Work in Europe* 2(3): 24-29.

Examines elder abuse in Ireland from the perspective of the construction of social problems. Gives an overview of general trends in recognition of family violence in Ireland with particular reference to developments in the field of elder abuse.

Perista, H. (1992) *Social and Economic Policies for Older People in Portugal*, Lisbon: GESIS.

Pijl, M. (1992) 'Netherlands policies for elderly people', *Social Policy and Administration* 26(3): 201-208.

Considers the development of policies for elderly people in the Netherlands.

Platz, M., and Petersen, N. F. (1992) *Social and Economic Policies for Older People in Denmark,* Copenhagen: National Institute of Social Research.

Ripamonti, E. (1995) 'Abuse against the elderly in Italy: a hidden phenomenon', *Social Work in Europe* 2(3): 15-17.

The most common family structure in Italy has, for centuries, been the so-called 'patriarchal' or 'extended family'. This type of family structure has guaranteed adequate support of two or three generations and, thus, the needs of the grandparents. However, the number of elderly in Italy, particularly in the north, is growing considerably in proportion to youth and networks of family and friends are being reduced. This article identifies an increased acknowledgement of elder abuse in Italy and looks at how it is perceived by the family and care institutions.

Scherman, K. G. (1995) 'Major changes in Sweden's pension system', *Ageing International* 22(2): 27-31.

Describes the current system, problems thereof, and the basic features of the new system.

Schmal, W. (1993) 'The '1992 reform' of public pensions in Germany: main elements and some effects', *Journal of European Social Policy* 3(1): 39-51.

This article gives an overview of central aspects (aims and measures) of the German Pension Reform Act of 1989, implemented in 1992. One main element is the redefinition of the pension adjustment procedure aimed at a constant net pension level. It is integrated in a self-regulating mechanism making financing a dependent variable. Other important measures are aimed at increasing the average retirement age and introducing a partial pension into social insurance. The article discusses possible economic effects of these measures as well as consequences of their introduction in East Germany after the German unification, taking into account the quite different situations in the East and West Germany.

Schumenn, J. (1988) 'Social services and social work practice with the elderly in the Federal Republic of Germany', *Journal of Gerontological Social Work* 12(1-2): 61-76.

The aged constitute a heterogeneous group; its members are distinguished by various circumstances of life. Yet, they are linked by one common factor, their age, and by the problems that arise from it. On the whole, senior citizens in our society are confronted with unfavourable structural conditions in comparison with other groups. These are caused by age-specific problems and, at the same time, by an insufficient provision of social facilities. Furthermore, they meet with disadvantages resulting from restricted access to infra-structural facilities as well as to the existing systems of social security. These disadvantages are described here.

Sinclair, I. (1988) 'Social work and personal social services for the elderly in Great Britain', *Journal of Gerontological Social Work* 12(1/2): 77- 92.

Interest in the elderly has been reinforced by three demographic trends. First, the number of pensioners is increasing: the 7.2 million pensioners in Great Britain in 1961 will have increased to 10.1 million by the year 2001. Second, this increase is particularly marked in the older age groups: during the same period the number aged 85 or over will increase from 300,000 to 1 million. Third, old people are increasingly unlikely to be living in situations where others in the home can look after them: between 1961 and 1981 the number of pensioners living alone has roughly doubled, while other social trends, in divorce and in employment expectations and geographical mobility of women, raise questions about the future availability of the traditional caregivers for the old. These figures fuel concern about the welfare of old people and the costs of looking after them.

Stahlberg, A-C. (1995) 'Pension reform in Sweden', *Scandinavian Journal of Social Welfare* 4(4): 267-273.

Pension reform has been placed on the political agenda in many countries. The Swedish parliament has decided to make significant changes in the pension system. This article presents the Swedish pension reform, which goes further than the changes in other European countries. According to the reforms, there will be a guaranteed pension that redistributes life-cycle incomes from rich to poor and an income-related actuarial pension without any intra- and intergenerational redistributive effects (with a few exceptions). The idea is to have an actuarial contribution-defined pension within a pay-as-you-go system.

Sundstrom, G. (1988) 'Social work and old age care in Sweden', *Journal of Gerontological Social Work* 12(1-2): 167-84.

No other country has proportionally as many old people in its population as Sweden. Large numbers of opinion polls, in Sweden and elsewhere, consistently show impressive support for old age care, both in public and private forms. Even when taxes collected for this purpose are explicitly juxtaposed to costs for child care in general, a majority of the population - from the age of 30 and onwards - favours old age care over child care. These findings may be interpreted differently, but the fact remains that public support of pensions, health care, and other provisions is widespread and firmly rooted in the policies of all political parties. Interestingly, Swedish political parties differ very little on this issue, with no shift in policy even today when approximately 33% of the GNP is spent on social security and, on an average, half of personal income disappears into taxes. By comparison, the

United States spends about 13% of its GNP on various forms of social security.

Sundstrom, G. and Malmberg, B. (1996) 'The long arm of the welfare state shortened: home help in Sweden', *Scandinavian Journal of Social Welfare* 5(2): 69-75.

Old age care in Sweden expanded greatly in all areas in the 1960s and 1970s. In the 1980s, both institutional and in-home services have retreated. Little substitution between the two kinds of care can be observed. Cutbacks relative to demographic needs, and probably also to actual needs, have occurred nationally and locally. Home help is analysed as a metaphor for social services and welfare at large. The strategy has been to give priority to the frailest and oldest clients. Others often have to make do without any services. Also, current recipients of home help services now get different inputs: in the 1980s and earlier, 8 of 10 home help hours were used for homemaking (such as shopping, cooking, cleaning and laundry); in the 1990s about half is used for personal care of clients.

Thane, P. (1987) *Economic Burden or Benefit? A Positive View of Old Age*, London: Centre for Economic Policy Research.

Tester, S. (1994) 'Implications of subsidiarity for the care of older people in Germany', *Social Policy and Administration* 28(3): 251-262.

Examines definitions and origins of the principle of subsidiarity and its application to welfare systems of the Federal Republic of Germany (FRG) with particular reference to the care of older people. the German corporatist welfare system is influenced by conservative views about status relations and Catholic teachings on family responsibilities. Since unification of Germany in 1990 new care systems based on the principle of subsidiarity have been imposed in eastern Germany. The FRG's social insurance system is based on entitlement benefits for those fully employed, while women and marginalised groups with low status in the labour market are poorly covered by insurance and may have to rely on stigmatising means-tested social welfare based on subsidiarity. Access to pluralist, fragmented care services depends on eligibility for funding through insurance or social welfare or else on ability to pay. Social care is poorly developed because of the emphasis on insurance and the medical model as well as on the principles of subsidiarity and self help which place an explicit duty on the family, mainly women, to care.

Thompson, J. (1987) 'Ageing of the population: contemporary trends and issues', *Population Trends*, (Winter): 18-22.

Walker, A. (1992) *Social and Economic Policies for Older People in the United Kingdom,* Sheffield: University of Sheffield.

Social work education

Barr, H. and Curl, D. (1994) 'The Swedish connection', *Issues in Social Work Education* 14(1): 83-97.

Through Nottingham University, Umea University in the north of Sweden sent seven social work students to Derbyshire for their final practice placements. This article describes their experience, that of their practice teachers and tutor, identifying lessons for the future.

Casino, E.S. (1983) 'Consultants and competence in the development of cross cultural Programs' in Landis, D. and Brislin, R (eds) *Handbook of Intercultural Training (Volume 2),* New York: Pergamon.

Cave, C. and Nichols, J. (1994) 'Can talking a different language work in training?', *Social Work in Europe* 1(3): 42-44.

Brief notes on working in Spain, across social and professional cultures and using a translator.

Christodoulou, C. (1991) 'Racism: a challenge to social work education and practice: The British experience', *Journal of Multicultural Social Work* 1(2): 99-106.

Traces the history of race relations in Great Britain. Discusses the recent rise of racism in Europe and the efforts of anti-racist groups. Outlines three models of anti-racist and multicultural social work education, and recommends continuing education and training for social workers in racism awareness.

Dominelli, L. (1996) 'The future of social work education', *Scandinavian Journal of Social Welfare* 5(3): 194-201.

Espwall, M. (1996) 'Development of knowledge in social work', *Nordisk Sosialt Arbeid* 16(4): 283-293.

The aim of this study was to investigate the development of knowledge in the subject of social work in Sweden in relation to its practical benefit and to scholarly rules and methods. The study is based on an analysis of all Swedish articles published in this journal, focusing mainly on issues such as research fields, characteristics of the authors, and the works referred to. Discusses findings.

Everett, R. D. (1990) 'Selling social work education 2' *Social Work Education* 9(1): 14-23.

Freed, A. O. (1995) 'Bulgarian social services and social work education', *International Social Work* 38(1): 39-51.

This article describes the changes taking place in Bulgaria in social welfare, social services, and social work education as an example of the transformations in process in the current transition from Communism to democratic, market-economy societies in Central and Eastern Europe. The previous paternalistic, centralized, excessively politicized system and services are being re-evaluated and restructured to meet the new economic needs and social demands brought about by privatization and shrinking government budgets. The existence of poverty, which as denied during Communism, is now being acknowledged and tackled. Some previous services are being reduced or dropped; new ones are being created; some very small private volunteer agencies are being established; and a new curriculum for social work education in universities is being developed. However, the rigidities of thinking fostered by fifty years of Communism must be overcome in order that substantial changes can take place.

Gould, H and Harris, A. (1996) 'Student imagery of practice in social work and teacher education: A comparative research approach', *British Journal of Social Work* 26(2): 223-237.

Within the fields of adult and professional education, the last ten years have seen the development of the reflective learning paradigm. This refutes a technical-rational model of the relationship between theory and practice, and proposes that practitioner knowledge is experientially constructed and organised through the schemata of imagery and metaphor. This paper outlines some findings from a comparative research study of social work and teaching students which adopted a phenomenological approach to understanding the self-imagery of student practitioners and its relationship to prior experience. Some implications for social worker education are considered, including the concept of 'imaginisation' - derived from post modernist organisational theory - as a strategy for empowerment.

Hämäläinen, J. (1989) 'Social pedagogy as a meta theory of social work education', *International Social Work* 32(2): 117-28.

Humphries, B. (1997) 'Reading social work: competing discourses in the rules and requirements for the diploma in social work', *British Journal of Social Work* 27(5): 641-658.

> The changes which have taken place across all of social work education and practice in Britain introduce a new phase for the profession in line with wider political and economic changes in the UK. The rules and requirements for the Diploma in Social Work exemplify these changes, and the document containing them is a useful focus for an analysis of what is at stake. This article employs discourse analysis to examine the ideological functions of the DipSW regulations and their relationship to wider social discourses, having in mind both the disciplining role of discourse and its possibilities for transformation. It identifies a dominant regulatory discourse and an oppositional liberatory discourse which are in dialogue with each other and with related discourse. The article considers the construction of social work in the document in its surveillance, managerialist, competence-based functions. The analysis also looks for contradictory voices in these discourses and in CCETSW's Welsh language policy and equal opportunities statement, which might offer sites of resistance and refusal. It is argued \that the shape of the stage social work has entered into is not inevitable, and the destabilising potential of such an analysis creates a space for the imagination of alternatives.

Jack, R. and Mosley, S. (1997) 'The client group preferences of diploma in social work students', *British Journal of Social Work* 27(6): 893-912.

> Social work is undergoing fundamental changes in terms of the way it is organised and how it is practised. If, in this shifting scenario of occupational deconstruction, the output of social work education is to be relevant to the work force needs welfare agencies - no matter how organised - it is important to know more about the client group preferences of social work students and what factors influence them. This longitudinal study inquired into student preferences at the beginning and end of three Diploma in Social Work programmes and its findings suggest that the socio-demographic characteristics of students are less demonstrably influential than previous experience and placement experience whilst on the programmes. In addition, students attribute far less influence to lectures and tutorials as change agents than they do

to placements, service users or other students. The implications of this for social work education are discussed.

Jones, S. (1998) 'The development of training of social pedagogues in Lithuania: a report of a needs analysis', *Issues in Social Work Education* 18(1): 60-81.

This paper describes some aspects of work resulting from a TEMPUS Project which was designed to undertake the development of a training model for the profession of a social pedagogue in one of the Baltic States. An initial needs analysis was conducted and the results are reported, and reflected upon. Issues are explored concerning the move towards a shared understanding of the role, functions and training requirements in the context of differential European approaches to social work and social pedagogy.

King, J. (1990) 'An olympic struggle', *Community Care* 834: 20-23.

Social work education in Greece.

Kopriva, K., and Tosner, J. (1996) 'Letter from Prague', *Social Work in Europe* 3(2): 16-17.

Describes a pilot project which aims to establish a regional training centre for social workers in the Czech Republic. Reports on a visit to London to meet social workers, teachers, officials and managers. Provides observations about social work in England which should not be regarded as more than preliminary impressions.

Lindstrom, M. (1993) 'Computers in teaching in Danish social work schools: the past and the present', *New Technology in the Human Services* 7(1) Summer: 26-28.

Argues that whilst other subjects have not been introduced to the social work curriculum before a lengthy discussion of the weight the subjects should have, how exams should be held and so forth, computers have found their way into the social work curriculum without such a process taking place. Considers the experiences in Denmark.

Lopez-Blasco, A. (1998) 'The development of social pedagogy in Spain: the tension between social needs, political response and academic interest', *European Journal of Social Work* 1(1): 41-53.

Provides a background to social work practice, research and education in Spain.

Majewska-Galeziak, A. (1998) 'Educating for social work in Poland - challenges of the transformation period', *European Journal of Social Work* 1(1): 95-100.

This article discusses the changing approach to social welfare staff education against a background of political and social transformation in Poland.

Mellor, M.J., Solomon, R., and Roughton, H. (1994) 'Geriatric social work education' (Rev.), *Ageing and Society* 14(3): 471-473.

Nelson, B. (1994) 'Social work training in Turkey', *Social Work in Europe* 1(2): 64.

Very brief notes on social work education in Turkey.

Ploem, R. (1994) 'The ecological perspective in Dutch tutoring and supervision', *Social Work in Europe* 1(3): 46-50.

Describes how the ecological perspective, described in social work by Germain and Hartman in the 1970s, can be used in tutoring /supervising social work students, providing the tutor/ supervisor and the student with a realistic view of the circumstances in which the learning process on the placement will take place.

Rafferty, J. (1997) 'Critical commentary: shifting paradigms of information technology in social work education and practice', British *Journal of Social Work* 27(6): 959-970.

Reznicek, I. (1994) 'Social work education at Czech Universities: the new beginnings' *Issues in Social Work Education* 14(1): 71-82.

Social policy and social work education in the Czech Republic are undergoing systemic transformation. Social policy is moving from universalism toward corporativsm or residualism and social work practice begins to adapt to these changes. Education in social work, until 1990 preserved at only post-secondary level has returned to universities. Curricula designs are being inspired by Anglo-Saxon and Central European examples from which the Czech educators select elements that fit their traditions and capacities. Briefly summarises the first experiences with social work teaching at university departments of sociology.

Robinson, E. (1993) 'Some psychological themes in social work education - a black perspective', *Social Work Education* 12(2): 29.

Social work education is currently undergoing major changes in professional training. The Central Council for Education and Training in Social Work (CCETSW) requirements for the Diploma in Social Work award attach a high priority to an anti-discriminatory approach in college and placement teaching and assessment. This area is now recognised as of central importance to the social worker's role and practice.

Rodrigues, F. (1990) 'Social work education: a view from Portugal', *Issues in Social Work Education* 10(1and2): 156-73.

This paper covers some topics considered important in the teaching of social work in Portugal. It includes information on the antecedents of social work teaching as it exists in its present version in Portugal; references to some areas of study and to problems related to them; and an explorative analysis of topics and questions that deal with the teaching of social work in Portugal with regard to the years ahead.

Ronnby, A. (1990) 'Teaching social work', *International Social Work* 33(4): 299-309.

Describes reform of the social work education curriculum in Sweden, aiming at a model which integrates theoretical and practice concerns.

Shardlow, S. M. and Doel, M. (1992) 'Social work education in Czechoslovakia', *Social Work Education* 11(2): 60.

Sluiters, S. (1992) 'Part-time education for social workers in Holland: historical developments and teaching methods', *Applied Community Studies* 1(3): 31-40.

A system of part-time education for social workers in Holland is described. It originated in emergency training courses for social services workers without training after the 1939-1945 war, and developed into a system of courses providing part-time learning for 'second-chance' and career change students over 25. Students worked, often in recent years as volunteers in self-help agencies rather than in conventional social services settings. A system of reflexive learning, based on project education and practice research projects developed from the work of Freire allowed students to bring work experience to the course and apply theoretical learning effectively. The extended period of work allied with learning allowed students to gain perspectives in their learning which is not available in training systems such as that in the UK with relatively short practice placements. However, problems in linking the agencies and educational institutions have presented difficulties.

Taylor, I. (1993) 'A case for social work evaluation of social work education', *British Journal of Social Work* 23(2): 123-138.

Thomas, T. (1990) 'Social work education: the Danish experience', *Social Work Education* 9(3): 31-35.
Describes the organisation of social work education in Denmark.

Social work: general issues

Ayala, L. (1994) 'Social needs, inequality and the welfare state in Spain: trends and prospects', *Journal of European Social Policy* 4(3): 159-179.
Public effort in social expenditure grew in Spain during the 1980s while in other countries there were sizeable cuts. The historical delay in the development of social protection and the desire to enlarge its coverage and adequacy helped to narrow the gap between the Spanish and European welfare states. The results are a reduction of poverty and some improvements towards less inequality. However, at the beginning of the 1990s the usual economic restrictions of a period of stagnation have led to a deep discussion about possible reductions in the process of uprating benefits, and abandoning the emphasis on universal and egalitarian income maintenance schemes. This has created a favourable ambience for privatisation strategies and the expansion of private provisions of pensions or health car. The ideological reply suffered by most contemporary welfare states has thus arrived also in Spain, although the system has still not reached adulthood. The objective of this article is to examine the main trends in income distribution and social protection developments in Spain, and try to foresee the potential incidence of social expenditure cuts.

Baker, J. (1994) 'Social protection in France: history and prospects for the 1990's', in Page, R. and Baldock, J. *Social Policy Review 6*, Social Policy Association.

Barberet, R., Barrett, D. and O'Neill, M. (1995) 'Young people and prostitution: no respecter of boundaries in North Western Europe', *Social Work in Europe* 2(2): 44-45.
Brief notes on prostitution and youth prostitution in Spain.

Bauer, R. and Popp, R. (1992) *Meeting people's needs in Germany*, London: Directory of Social Change.

Berglind, H., Gullberg, A., Eloffson, S. (1996) 'Work or welfare - a dilemma in the declining Swedish welfare state', *Scandinavian Journal of Social Welfare* 5(3): 148-153.

The number of welfare recipients among people of working age increased from 1985 to 1992 in Sweden. Unexpectedly, this increase also took place under the economic boom during the late 1980s, characterised by very low unemployment. This is shown in a study of a sample of the Swedish population. Not only has the number if welfare recipients increased, there has been a parallel increase in the relative number of people who are gainfully employed. This trend prevails until 1991, when the unemployment rates start going down. Until then, the development is characterised by growing polarisation into those who depend on work for their subsistence and those who depend on transfer payments from the welfare system. The development of welfare dependence has been different for men and women. The reasons for this development are discussed. Data about the increasing cost of social security are also presented, showing that the welfare system has not been in any immediate economic crisis from 1985 to 1993.

Bergmark, A. (1997) 'From reforms to rationing? Current allocative trends in social services in Sweden', *Scandinavian Journal of Social Welfare* 6(2): 74-81.

Looks at the consequences of economic constraints on social services in Sweden. Raises concerns of resource allocation, starting with an outline of the impact of economic developments on different sectors of the social services. Focuses on recent developments and strategies for managing financial cut-backs are discussed in detail.

Brinkman, J. (1998) 'Social work for refugees: overcoming trauma and cultural differences', *Social Work in Europe* 5(1): 21-24.

Provides a brief outline of the position of refugees in the Netherlands and of the background to their problems. Describes some of the problems that carers experience in their work with refugees and elaborates on some theoretical considerations which offer a basis for work across cultural boundaries. Concludes by offering some guidelines for working with refugees.

Cannan, C. (1996) 'The impact of social development and anti-exclusion policies on the French social work professions', *Social Work in Europe* 3(2): 1-4.

French social work is undergoing a profound change in its 'classical mission', a change directed by national social policies emphasising the drive against exclusion and by the local interpretations of this in the cities, departments (counties) and agencies. To a British eye, a whole new field of community development work is opening up, providing huge opportunities for the profession to rediscover and to demonstrate that strand in its history and identity. This article is based on visits to a department in northwest France over a number of years. Describes the local implementation of national policies by interviewing social workers, their managers, and social worker trainers and sociologists.

CCETSW (1999) *Social Work and Social Change In Northern Ireland: Issues for Contemporary Practice*, Belfast: Central Council for Training and Education in Social Work.

Chytil, O. (1998) 'Social work in the Czech Republic', *Social Work in Europe* 5(3): 48-55.

This paper overviews the total transformation of Czechoslovakian society: in economic, political and social-political terms.

Cohen, P. (1990) 'Going Dutch', *Social Work Today* 22(9): 15-17.

Concerned by rising demand for and costs of residential care, social work in the Netherlands is moving towards a mixture of residential and domiciliary care to best meet the user's need.

Cooper, C. (1999) 'Empowering practice in social care: lessons from Swedish housing', *Social Work in Europe* 6(1): 14-22.

This article explores some of the preconditions for effective user involvement in social services, achieved through an examination or residents' democracy in the Swedish housing system. Argues that by exploring housing, where participatory structures are more generally developed, we can establish important generalisations for the design of involvement structures in other services.

Dobelniece, S. (1994) 'The poverty line and subsistence minimum in Latvia', *Scandinavian Journal of Social Welfare* 3(4): 193-202.

This article gives a picture of the difficulties of defining poverty and setting up a poverty line in a post-Communist country in the period of transition to democracy and a market economy. The ongoing processes are linked with the deterioration of living standards and wellbeing of the population. The government has attempted to protect the population socially, accepting a subsistence minimum and later a crisis subsistence minimum. It is difficult to argue that the activities of the government have been successful and helped much in improving the living standards of the population of Latvia.

Doel, M. and Shardlow, S. M. (1990) 'Bok, Wotcha et Salut!' *Social Work Today* 21(19): 32.

Envall, E. (1996) 'Challenges for social work in the future', *Nordisk Sosialt Arbeid* 16(2): 83-93.

This article is an abridged version of a paper presented to the Nordic seminar 'Poverty and Expulsion - Strategies for Social Work', held in Oslo in March 1996. Based on the conditions for doing social work in the Third World, the author draws parallels to mechanisms of marginalisation and expulsion ion the Swedish welfare state today. The thesis is that, by knowing the historical roots of social work and by having a more global view of the situation of other colleagues, one can understand one's own situation better and act better. Finally, the author attempts a definition of social work by retelling the story of 'The Imman and the Eighteenth Camel': the social worker is a passer-by who is not part of the system who makes his or her contribution without adding or subtracting anything.

Ganssmann, H. (1993) 'After unification: problems facing the German welfare state', *Journal of European Social Policy* 3(2): 79-90.

The transition of East Germany from a socialist socio-economic system to the western combination of capitalism, liberal democracy and the welfare state is examined in the perspective of potential lessons for other such transition processes in Eastern Europe. The focus is on the way in which welfare state institutions as they have evolved in West Germany can be used to cope with the labour market problems which have emerged in East Germany. It is argued that the general nature of West German welfare state programmes is patterned by the insurance principle and that their corresponding normative foundation is not suitable to achieve the integration of East Germans into a German society formed by the institutions of former West Germany, even if enormous economic resources are used to cushion the transition process.

Gould, A. (1988) *Conflict and Control in Welfare Policy: The Swedish Experience*, Harlow: Longman.

Examines the conflict between welfare and control in a Swedish context. Uses children in care; 'social assistance', and drug addiction, alcohol abuse and AIDS as case studies.

Grevot, A. (1996) 'The changing role of Associations in French social welfare', *Social Work in Europe* 3(2): 5-7.

The transfer of control in 1983 of most statutory social work services in France from central government to the Conseil General (the equivalent of British county councils) has substantially affected the relationship between public authorities and the Associations (the French voluntary sector). Associations are a large component of the French social welfare system and this is reflected in the major role they play in the life of the community as a whole.

Habermann, U. (1993) 'Why groupwork is not put into practice: reflections on the social work scene in Denmark', *Groupwork* 6(1): 17-29.

Considers the reasons why social groupwork is rarely used by Danish social workers.

Hardeman, W. (1994) 'Dutch move carefully towards service-user sovereignty', *Care Plan* 1(1): 19.

Describes an experiment in budget control by service users.

Hare, I. (1993) New Developments in Hungarian Social Work, Washington DC: NASW.

Harris, J. (1994) 'Evolution across two revolutions: social care policy in Czechoslovakia', *Critical Social Policy* 40 (Summer): 70-87.

This article begins by noting the increasing appeal of 'two breaks' accounts of post-war developments in Central and Eastern Europe. The universal applicability of such accounts is questioned through an examination of general trends in social care policy in (the former) Czechoslovakia, an examination which stresses a gradual process of policy change across the revolutions of 1948 and 1989. The prospects for pluralist social care policies, espoused across the period of the Velvet Revolution, are than assessed in terms of: their political ramifications; the strains they will place on the informal sector; the trend in divorce rates; the impact of economic policy; the potential contribution of the voluntary and commercial sectors;

and the role of the state. The article concludes with a tentative consideration of the implications this general review of social care policy in one country may have for the study of comparative social policy.

Harris, J. (1997) 'Past patterns, present prospects: social work in the Czech republic', *International Social Work* 40(4): 425-432.

Social work in the Czech Republic has a history stretching back to the establishment of the (then) Czechoslovak State. Shortly after the founding of Czechoslovakia in 1918, the Higher School for Social Care was established. In the inter-war years, the strong social democratic influence within the permanent parliamentary coalition favoured the development of social work. Under state socialism, social work survived, despite the official 'line' being maintained that social problems were a characteristic of capitalist societies. In the Communist Party's rhetoric the all embracing meeting of needs would render social work redundant. However, two forms of social work continued within the framework of state socialism.

Hesser, K.E. H. and Koole, W. (eds) (1994) *Social work in the Netherlands: current developments*, Amsterdam: Hogeschool van Amsterdam. Faculty of Social Work.

Introduces social work in the Netherlands and goes on to look at: social work and drug addiction - the Amsterdam model; female social work or gender-specific social work with women and girls; gender-specific social work with men and boys; the office for children of drug addicted parents; Opstap, a preventive home based programme; social work with people with learning difficulties, older people, migrants, people with mental health problems, and young people; AIDS prevention; community development; child welfare; and an overview of social work education in the Netherlands.

Imbrogno, S. (1990) 'Social policy planning and social work practices in Poland', *Social Work* 35: 302-306.

Poland's social welfare system has improved steadily; building on socialist ideology of a universal health and social insurance programme. The author discusses advancements in social work knowledge and research methods in professional social work practices. These developments contrast with the periodic economic crises and the absence of basic consumer goods and services. The situation is examined in the context of social norms of the socialist system and its policy outcomes, the structural arrangements for implementing human services, and the behaviour of voluntary agencies acting autonomously on behalf of constituents.

Jarre, D. (1991) 'Subsidiarity in social services provision in Germany', *Social Policy and Administration* 25(3): 211-217.

Explains the concept of subsidiarity and the way in which it regulates the practice of the German social welfare system and social services provision and the relationship between statutory bodies and voluntary organisations.

Julkunen, I. (1994) *Social assistance in Finland*, Helsinki: National Research and Development Centre for Welfare and Health.

Kaarlainen, J. (1997) 'The production of "criminals" in Finland in the 1980s', Scandinavian Journal of Social Welfare 6(1): 61-67.

This article describes from the constructionist starting-point the quantitative development of people sentenced to prison for the first time in the 1980s in Finland. The reasons for and consequences of this development are also examined. The data consist of a register that covers all the decisions given by the Finnish lower courts of justice for the period 1977-1991. The basic observation is that the number of Finnish people defined for the first time as "criminals" decreased by about 20% in the 1980s. However, at the same time the penal system has increased its efficiency: the number of registered crimes and sentences has grown considerably. This has led to a more rapid circulation of "criminals" between prison and the outside. At the same time, the death rate of those labelled as criminals has increased in all age groups, which indicates the growing marginalisation of that diminishing group.

Katrougalos, G. S. (1996) 'The Southern European Welfare model: the Greek welfare state, in search of an identity', *Journal of European Social Policy* 6(1): 39-60.

The aim of the article is not to describe in detail the social protection system in Greece or in the other southern European countries. Its main ambition is to offer a general overview of its formation and an explanation for its particularities. The basic thesis is that essentially the Greek Welfare State belongs to the continental model. The conclusion of the author is that although there is a clear trend in the direction of convergence of the Greek welfare system with the median European standards, Greece still has a considerable lag to overcome.

Karvinen, S., Pösö, T. and Satka, M. (eds) (1999) *Reconstructing Social Work Research*, Jyväskylä, Finland: SoPhi.

This book includes a representative sample of social work research from Finland. It is specifically aimed at an international audience.

Keller, H. (1998) 'Multicultural professionalism and the identity of social work in Switzerland', *Social Work in Europe* 5(1): 17.

Keller initially shares some personal experiences concerning ideas of identity and culture. Secondly, he describes the nature of co-operation in Swiss society. Finally, Keller discusses the implications this has for the way their professional association functions and how they work together within it. This is a continually evolving process - particularly in relation to notions of culture and identity which constitute a central principal of social professions.

Koenis, S. (1999) 'The uses of social science in the history of Dutch social work, 1900-1980', *European Journal of Social Work* 2(1): 41-53.

In this article the author reviews the history of Dutch social work between 1900 and 1980 and tries to shed light on how Dutch social workers enlisted various insights developed by the social sciences to gain jurisdiction in dealing with social problems. Argues against the simplistic idea that scientific knowledge is merely 'applied' in practical settings such as social work.

Kovero, S. (1999) 'The moment of truth in Finnish social work?' *Social Work in Europe* 6(1): 40-45.

Provides a history of the development of social welfare policy and practice in Finland.

Kultygin, V.P. (1993) 'Poverty and social trends in Russia', *Scandinavian Journal of Social Welfare* 2(3): 142-149.

This article describes the socio-economic situation of the Russian population and its dynamics in 1992. The analysis is based on series of regional surveys led by the All-Russian Living Standards Research Centre and on official Russian statistical data. The basic unit of analysis is the family, and hence family typology found both in research and in practical social work is introduced. Besides describing and discussing the growing poverty tendencies in contemporary Russia, the article also contains methodological recommendations for social policy bodies and social workers on the strategy of work in social maintenance and social support of the least secure population strata.

Lawson, C. and Nemec, J. (1998) 'Central European health reform: the case of Slovakia, 1990-97', *Journal of European Social Policy* 8(3): 237-252.

This article focuses on changes in Slovak health-care policy 1990-97. Also compares these to recent Czech, Polish and Hungarian experiences.

Lévai, K. (ed.) (1999) *Progress Through Partnership*. Hungary: Social Innovation Foundation.

Lindholm, K. and Boklund, A. (1993) 'The Swedish Association for Social Work: 90 years of inspiration', *Scandinavian Journal of Social Welfare* 2(3): 102-103.

Loewenberg, F. M. (ed.) (1998) *Meeting the Challenges of a Changing Society: Fifty years of social work in Israel*. Jerusalem: The Hebrew University.

Lorenz, W. (1991) 'The new German children and young people act', *British Journal of Social Work* 21(4): 329-339.

Assesses the significance of the Act in the context of German social policy traditions and sums up the main sections.

Lorenz, W. (1994) 'Personal social services' in Clasen, J., and Freeman, R. (eds) *Social Policy in Germany*, London: Harvester Wheatsheaf.

Markopoulou, C. L. (1991) Social Services and Minority Groups in Greece: Attitudes and Ethnicity in Relation to the Application of Social Welfare Programmes, Unpublished PhD Theses, University of Sussex.

This thesis is about the provision of social services to ethnic minorities in Greece.

Martinez-Brawley, E. E. (1991) 'Social services in Spain: the case of rural Catalonia', *International Social Work* 34(3): 265-286.

Provides an overview of the Spanish social service system and describes the provision of social services in rural Catalonia, utilizing detailed field observations from two specific counties or 'comarcas' in the province of Girona. The research relied on observations of the daily activities of the local social workers, including home visits and client interviews. Interviews with local- and national-level government officials, local physicians, priests and other significant members of the helping community were also utilized. The study sought to assess the presence or absence of three major characteristics of rural service: generalism, localism and orientation to the community (Part II). Comments and descriptions are framed within the much broader context of the personal social services laws in Spain and the new political organization of Spain and Catalonia. Because of the paucity of literature written in English about the social services in Spain, a comprehensive overview of the legal framework for the social services is also included (Part I).

Moenaert, P. (1991) 'Cash and caring in Brugge', *Social Policy and Administration* 25(3): 202-210.

The remit of the Public Centre for Social Welfare in Brugge is to offer both financial support, social work help, help with employment and training and referral to other services.

Monk, V., and Singleton, N. (1995) 'Lessons from social work in the Czech Republic', *Social Work in Europe* 2(3): 42-48.

Cheshire County Council Social Services Department, and University College Salford School of Social Work, have recently been involved in establishing an EC funded project with the Social Care Departments of three Czech Local Authority Districts, the University of Hradec Kralove Social Work Department and the Irish Western Health Board. In this article, the authors discuss their observations on Czech social work and Czech society from two exploratory visits made to set up the project. Their observations include social policy and management issues, social work practice issues and future challenges facing social work in the Czech Republic.

Niesen, K. (1996) 'Violence, an inescapable part of the everyday life of the social worker', *Nordisk Sosialt Arbeid* 16(2): 106-113.

This article tries to enumerate the problems that a social worker faces in connection with violence and threats from clients. These problems have become obvious in Denmark after the murder of a social worker. The problems on which this article focuses are: what kind of violence do we meet as social workers; who commits the violence and what does it express; can preventative measures be taken at organisational level, among colleagues, and by the individual social worker; why do social workers become paralysed and accept violence? Also looks at the humility of the social worker in relation to the increased focus of the media on violence at workplace. Describes a large scale Danish development project entitled 'Violence as a form of expression - an educational challenge', which paints a broad picture of the experiences and results of a three-year nationwide project focusing on the social-educational sphere.

Olsson, S. (1987) 'Towards a transformation of the Swedish welfare state' in Friedmann, R.R., Gilbert, N. and Sherer, M. (eds) *Modern Welfare States: A Comparative View of Trends and Prospects*, London: Wheatsheaf.

Olsson, E. L., and Junghill, J. (1997) 'The practitioner and 'naive theory' in social work intervention processes', *British Journal of Social Work* 27(6): 931-950.

Research in social work has often taken for granted that methods of intervention in this area are well defined. Few studies analyse or give detailed descriptions of how the work is really constructed. This issue is explored, starting from the social worker's personal frame of reference. Eight categories of explanation and six different methods of intervention are here defined. Concludes that constitute important aspects of the interaction dynamics between social workers and their clients which need to be further investigate.

Olsson, O., et al. (1994) 'The prevalence of heavy narcotics abuse in Sweden in 1992', *Scandinavian Journal of Social Welfare* 3(2): 81-84.

A case-finding study was carried out in 1992 to determine the prevalence of drug abuse in Sweden. Several authorities in 100 local communities and 59 police districts were selected to participate in the case-finding research. The number of heavy drug abusers was estimated to be 17,000. Heavy drug use is defined as 'any intravenous use of drugs, regardless of substance, or any daily or near-daily use of drugs, regardless of the administration'. The study was designed to make the results comparable to a similar study in 1979 in which the number found was 12,000. According to the studies, the number of heavy drug abusers increased by 5000 between 1979 and 1992. The age distribution shows that the recruitment of abusers has declined, especially among young people.

Pecnik, N., Soroya, B., Stubbs, P. (1995) 'Sunflowers of hope: some issues in social work with refugees and displaced persons in Croatia', *Practice,* 7(2): 5-12.

Describes the work of 'Suncokret', a Non-Governmental Organisation working in refugee camps in Croatia. The focus is on the history, philosophy and objectives of 'Suncokret' and situates them in a broader political context. In the process, some issues concerning the provision of social work for vulnerable communities are addressed more generally.

Sanders, A. (1995) 'You have to start somewhere: report from Estonia' *Social Work in Europe* 2(1): 17-20.

Brief recollections from two visits to Estonia as guest of the universities of Tallinn and Tartu.

Saraceno, C. and Negri, N. (1994) 'The changing Italian welfare state', *Journal of European Social Policy* 4(1): 19-34.

Starting in 1990, a series of legislative measures have been re-shaping the Italian welfare state, as judged by the aims behind the reforms of the 1970s, which had defined social rights in the field of social and health services. At the same time, these changes have been redefining the roles, rights and duties of different actors involved: not only citizens, but also state, local government, service workers, trade unions, non- governmental organisations, and families. Behind these changes lie financial constraints, and increasing social dissatisfaction with the unfulfilled promises of the 1970s. This article briefly describes the main features and ambiguities of the social reforms of the 1970s and the role of NGOs in the history and organisation of the Italian welfare state, and analyses the present reformulation of the responsibilities and powers of local government, the new role of NGOs envisaged by recent legislation, and the features of the 'new' National Health Service and its possible social consequences.

Satka, M. (1993) 'Social service professionals in Finland under the pressures of a depressed economy and European integration', *Scandinavian Journal of Social Welfare* 2(4): 215-218.

The Nordic welfare states are known as women-friendly. However, during the last years their policies have been to turn the back on women. At least in Finland there seem to exist two powerful forces that have advanced the non- egalitarian development: the economic recession of the late 1990s and the integration of Europe. The decline of the Nordic welfare states is going to have considerable consequences for social service professionals, the great majority of whom are women. Therefore, they should create new strategies and find new allies in order to defend their own as well as their clients rights.

Schiele, J. H. (1996) 'Afro-centricity. An emerging paradigm in social work practice', *Social Work* 41 (3): 284-94.

Although several models of social work practice that can better assist people of colour have emerged, the cultural values of this population generally have not been used as a theoretical base to develop new practice models. This situation not only prevents a truly diversified theoretical base in social work but also reinforces the hegemony of Euro-centric concepts for explaining and solving human and societal problems. Recently, the concept 'Afrocentricity' has been used to describe the philosophical concepts of Afrocentricity as a social science paradigm on which social work practice can be conceived and built, and explains the reasons for the emergence of an Afrocentric social science perspective. Social workers are encouraged to embrace the Afrocentric paradigm because of its emphasis on eliminating oppression and spiritual alienation.

Sharlin, S. A. (1998) 'Soviet immigrants to Israel: users and non-users of social work services', *International Social Work* 41(4): 455-470.

Discusses how Israel has recently become home for about half a million immigrants from the former Soviet Union. Hardships of absorption, a different and strange culture, and the unfamiliar educational system that these immigrants have to content with lead to numerous personal and family problems. Discusses how soviet immigrants are unaccustomed to seeking and making use of social work services. Compares Soviet immigrants who do apply for social assistance with those who do not and makes some recommendations.

Sihvo, T., and Uusitalo, H. (1995) 'Attitudes towards the welfare state have several dimensions: evidence from Finland', Scandinavian *Journal of Social Welfare* 4(4): 215-223.

The dimensions and structures of opinions on the welfare state are not well known. This study distinguishes five dimensions based on previous literature: responsibility for welfare, financing of the welfare state, the use of benefits, the adequacy of the welfare state benefits and the effects of the welfare state. One or more attitude indicators are formed for each dimension by means of factor analysis of empirical material. Examination of the correlations between the dimensions and attitudes yields two opinion structures. A supportive attitude structure is founded on the concept that public authorities have responsibility for welfare services, a positive attitude towards public financing of welfare services, and on the concepts that the amount and quality of services and the level of income transfers is not adequate. The critical cluster of attitudes is formed by the reliance on private responsibility, negative attitude towards public financing and on the concepts that benefits are overused and that the welfare state makes its clients passive. Finally, the variation in attitudes among the population of Finland are studied by means of regression analysis. Social Class, age and political party sympathies are the most important explanatory factors for a range of attitudes.

Smith, A. and Kluz K. (1997) 'Social care in Poland: opportunities for the future', *International Social Work* 40(4): 451-465.

Analyses contemporary social problems in Poland, and offers social policy recommendations. Discusses the well-being of the population; societal goals; changing organisational structures, and the role of the social work profession in policy-making, programme administration and practice-based research, as well as in direct service.

Sobis, I. (1995) 'Unemployment in Poland - causes and remedial measures', *Scandinavian Journal of Social Welfare* 4(3): 151-161.

This article describes unemployment and labour market policy in Poland after 1989. The analysis is based on official statistics, legislation and Polish social science literature. The unemployment situation in Poland is continually changing. Conclusion drawn by social scientists in 1991 and 1992 no longer give an adequate account of labour market trends in 1995. Steeply rising unemployment is the most traumatic upheaval in the post-Communist Polish society. At the end of 1989, the number of people looking for work in Poland was far less than the number of available jobs. However, by the end of 1992 there were 62 job-seekers for every job opening, dropping to 56 in September 1994. The social consequences associated with unemployment vary from region to region. Women and young people predominate among the unemployed. The Polish government set up a work fund in January 1990 to alleviate unemployment. The Work Fund is the first real measure taken to assist the unemployed, but new legislation is needed if it is to become more effective.

Spicker, P. (1995) 'Inserting the excluded: the impact of the 'Revenu Minimum d'Insertion' on poverty in France', *Social Work in Europe* 2(2): 8-14.

The Revenu Minimun d'Insertion (RMI) in France is a residual income maintenance benefit, intended to cover the circumstances of people who are otherwise left out of the social security system. The benefit is conditional, however, on a 'programme of insertion', and claimants are required to make contracts, under the guidance of a social worker, which will lead to them being appropriately integrated into society. This is having an important effect on the pattern of social work in France, with some discomfort expressed by the social workers involved. In practice, the nature of the contracts is often unclear. The literature tends to emphasise their social role, but many are concerned in practice with employment. There are concerns that the effect of the provision may be to impede the delivery of benefits.

Svetlik, I. (1993) 'Reform of social policy in Slovenia: a soft approach', *Journal of European Social Policy* 3(3): 195-208.

Slovenia faces similar problems to other central European countries which have introduced radical reforms of their economic and political systems - in addition, it has become an independent state. However, its export- oriented and relatively well-developed economy has prevented the need for drastic cuts in welfare programmes or a reduction of public services to be replaced by services provided by the voluntary sector. This article describes major changes that have been introduced in the areas of employment, housing, health care, child care, education and poverty relief in the course of the last four years. In the final part of the article, main trends in social policy are discussed, which, it is argued, are rooted in the 1980s and remain under social and political control.

Szeman, S. and Gathy, V. (1993) 'The voluntary sector in the welfare mix: the Hungarian Maltese Charity Service', *Journal of European Social Policy* 3(2): 119-144.

Reviews the difficulties faced by Hungary in moving to a market economy and the effect on social policy and the welfare state. Various actors in the emerging welfare model are outlined, and one in particular - the Hungarian Maltese Charity Service, whose growth has been meteoric, is described in detail.

Tojcic, I. (1997) 'Unaccompanied refugee children from former Yugoslavia: consequences of community destruction in Bosnia', *Social Work in Europe* 4(3): 25-27.
Looks at the effects on children and young people exiled from Bosnia.

Tutvedt, D. and Young, L. (eds) (1991) Social Work and the Norwegian Welfare State, Oslo: NKSH.
Aims to introduce social work as practised within the Norwegian welfare state, outlining legislation and current problems.

Van Wormer, K. (1994) 'Privatisation in the social welfare state: the case of Norway', *Scandinavian Journal of Social Welfare* 3(1): 39-44.
The method of deviant case analysis is used to study privatisation under the least hospitable circumstances. Norway, a country steeped in principles of egalitarianism, is moving in new directions, mostly due to forces from the global economy. This article puts contemporary trends in sociocultural context. The implications for the health and mental health fields are discussed.

Vidmar, A.K. (1998) 'Social work in the workplace: A view from Slovenia', *Social Work in Europe* 5(1): 34-36.
In recent years Slovenia has experienced a double transition: an economic one from socialism to capitalism, and a political one from being one of the Republics in former Yugoslavia to an independent state. The transition to a market economy has - among other things - had a strong impact on the situation of employees and on the role of social workers in business enterprises and other organisations.

Visser, W. (1995) 'Confusion behind the dikes: chronic high unemployment in the Dutch welfare state', *Scandinavian Journal of Social Welfare* 4(3): 140-150.
Twenty years ago Dutch society was hit by a serious rise of unemployment that put the Dutch welfare state to the test: Should the welfare state be able to prevent unemployment to becoming high and chronic as in the 1930s? Should the welfare state be able to prevent mass poverty as in the 1930s? The answers are well known. The Dutch welfare state has not been able to forestall persistent high unemployment and, in fact, has more or

less produced a dual society although without producing mass poverty. This article goes out three issues related to these developments. A bird's-eye view is presented of the unemployment trajectory of the 1970s, 1980s and the first half of the 1990s; The position of the Netherlands relative to other counties in Europe is unfolded. Some issues concerning the effects of chronic unemployment on the functioning of the Dutch political economy are presented.

Voges, W. and Rohwer, G. (1992) 'Receiving social assistance in Germany: risk and duration', *Journal of European Social Policy* 2(3): 175-191?

Draws upon statistical data to evaluate the utilisation and duration of social assistance receipt in Germany, finding that dependency on social assistance is a relatively short-term situation in an individual's life- cycle. The same determinants which increase the probability of social assistance receipt (previous receipt of assistance, a sick or disabled person in the household, changes in household size, female gender) also appear to hinder its termination.

Walls, G. (1994) 'Actors, legitimation and cultures of social work', *Scandinavian Journal of Social Welfare* 3(4): 218-225.

This article is based on a study of rationality and language games in social work, focussing on the actors of social welfare and health care. Included are the heads and social workers of public welfare and health care agencies and institutions, officials of voluntary organisations, and activists in social change-oriented action groups in Finland.

Warzywoda-Kruszynska, W. and Grotowska-Leder, J. (1993) 'Poverty and social conditions in Poland during the transformation to a market economy', *Scandinavian Journal of Social Welfare* 2(3): 115-127.

The social welfare system in Poland was changed during the 1990s. The full employment policy, as a guarantee for social security, was abandoned and the institutions through which social resources were distributed were replaced. State-owned enterprises previously fulfilled certain social functions; the necessary resources came from state subsidies and from obligatory funds: housing and social funds as well as a proportion of wage costs. Thus, the prices of many types of important consumption goods (such as food and housing) were fixed at a relatively low level. The elimination of such subsidies resulted in the bankruptcy of many state-owned enterprises which in turn, led to the diminished importance of the social security function of industrial enterprises. Their role in the newly created social welfare system was taken over by social welfare centres, through which assistance was distributed to those in need. Besides, the traditional recipients of social assistance, a growing number of unemployed people, who comprise approximately 14% of the productively active citizens, have also begun collecting assistance.

Zorc, D. (1994) 'Slovene youth in a period of transition from the Socialist system to a modern European state', *Social Work in Europe* 1(3): 14-17.
Describes how the transition from socialism has affected Slovenian youth.

Social Work Dictionaries

The search did not generate any information about social work dictionaries to assist with translation across two or more languages. However, the following may be helpful:

Books that define concepts in social work in English.

Dearling, A. (1993) *Social Welfare Word Book*, London: Longman.

Thomas, M., and Pierson, J. (1995) *Dictionary of Social Work*, London: Collins Educational.

Timms, N., and Timms, R. (1982) *A Dictionary of Social Welfare*, London: Routledge and Kegan Paul.

Books that provide translations of social work terms between two or more languages.

Berger, P-A. and Kühne, K. (1996) *Schweizer Wöterbuch fürden Sozialbereich/Lexique Suisse du domaine social*, Köniz: Edition Soziothek.
Translation between French and German

Kahl, W., and Bradley, G. (Eds.) (1994) *Dictionary for Social Professions*, Frankfurt am Main: Fachhochschulverlag, Frankfurt am Main.
Translation between English and German. Includes a disk version

Zapf, K. (1961) *Dictionary of Social Work*, Köln: Carl Heymanns Verlag KG.
Translation between Dutch, English, French, Greek German, Italian, Spanish.

Index